Let's Get Real
No Filter Needed

POLLY HERRIN

Copyright © 2021 POLLY HERRIN

All rights reserved.

ISBN: 9798763316032

A Note From Polly

It's a serious challenge to find authenticity in this filtered world. Social media has duped us into believing our value is found in the likes of many, so we do as we see, and we seek perfection. Anything less than perfect, we filter. Since when was it not good enough to just be exactly who God made you? Who convinced us a perfect performance is needed to be perfectly loved and filters are required to be beautiful? More insanely crazy is this idea that if you mess up you become disqualified forever. <u>Lies, all lies!</u> The enemy has been a liar since day one, and with twisted truths and deceitful arguments, he seeks to dismantle your relationship with God. He knows full well, before your Creator, you can unveil your flawed life, and still be loved.

God is crazy in love with the *REAL* you, the imperfect you, the chaotic you, the sometimes crazy you, and even the faithless you. He loves you on your good days and on your worst day. His love allows messy and growing seasons. It never waivers, nor is it fickle or indecisive. It is steadfast, unmovable, and extremely extravagant. His love is perfect and He loves the imperfect! Once you experience this amazing love, you won't settle for conditional love!

It's time to burn the badges of shame and guilt that have kept you from becoming all God said you could be. Even with the scars you bear and the mistakes you've made, you can still take your place in the Kingdom. <u>**You belong here!**</u> However, don't be shocked if you irritate the *religious folks* who will suggest you need to improve yourself before you take a position in His community. Resist the urge to embrace their sinister opinions, and allow your heart to be transformed by God, however long that takes! And the best benefit to living *real*, is just maybe your unfiltered life will encourage others to know and believe, God still loves them too.

If you're looking for perfection, you won't find it here. I am far less than perfect. I don't have a perfect marriage, but I am happily married to my college sweetheart. I love my kids, they are my greatest gifts, but they aren't perfect either. I haven't been the perfect mother, or daughter, the perfect wife, friend or leader. **Unfiltered, I am far less than perfect and still loved by God! I absolutely know if God can bring goodness, restoration, and lasting fruit through my life, He will do the same for you. God has not changed His mind about you, He's just waiting for you to change your mind about yourself.**

May His excessive, unconditional, transcending love, catapult you into all things beautiful and restored.

I'm cheering you on,

Polly

- Promise you will commit to finishing the book. Girl, see I am already speaking the truth to somebody. Some of you need a finisher's anointing, and I pray you receive it. Whenever you set out to make strides forward the enemy will always attempt to detour you with distractions. Let's not let him win this time.

- I intentionally organized each devotional to include a scripture to memorize. God's words have all authority and the power to do what nothing else can. Commit to memorizing the scriptures!

- Purchase a copy of the book for a friend(s). If a book betters you in anyway, it will most likely do the same for those you endear. Gift one to a friend, and together in a small group setting, use this devotional as a starting point to work through false strongholds. I can't wait to hear about it.

- Pray the prayers and say the declarations out-loud. Jesus promises whatever you ask in prayer, **believe that you have received it**, and it will be yours (Mark 11:24). *What a promise!*

- I believe God can use a book to transform a life. It's happened to me many times. It doesn't even have to be a great book, it can just be well-timed for the season. I pray you allow a "pause" in your life to let God speak what He desires to say through these devotionals. Don't rush Him.

✸ Use the **#LetsGetReal** *hashtag* to share your thoughts and insights on social media. Repost a quote, give new insights about the devotional, or add your small group discussions. Be sure to tag me (info below) on those posts so I can share them too. Together we can give encouragement to others.

Let's go! I can't wait to take this journey with you.

To host Polly at your next event please send your requests and inquiries to: connect.pollyherrin@gmail.com

    Instagram: @pollyherrin33
    Facebook: Polly Stegall Herrin
    Email: connect.pollyherrin@gmail.com

#1
NO FILTER NEEDED

People may not let you back in, but God will! - Polly Herrin

Do you believe with unrelenting confidence Jesus loves you? Are you convinced His pursuit of you won't end because of your bad choices and messy mistakes? I hope to convince you we cannot be unloved by Jesus, because Love is not just something He does, it's who He is!

A story of betrayal, revenge, and scandalous sin begins in Genesis chapter twenty-eight. The main character is a girl whose name is Tamar and I doubt you will ever forget her.

Tamar, was a young woman married to Er, who was Judah's eldest son. Er was so wicked that God killed him and left Tamar a widow. Desperately wanting children, she married her brother-in-law Onan. According to Levirate law, a widow was encouraged to marry any brothers in the household of her deceased husband in order to produce children. You're not going to believe this . . . the Bible tells us Onan was also wicked and God killed him too. *You'll have to go read the details in your Bible. It's really to graphic for me to describe here. (I'm blushing.)*

Judah had one more son named Shelah. Don't you think Tamar was a little skeptical by now wondering if he would also turn out to be a wicked man? It didn't matter because Shelah was too young to marry. Judah sent Tamar back to her hometown with a promise that when Shelah was old enough he would allow them to marry, but unfortunately, Judah never kept his promise. Tamar was heartbroken and publicly disgraced. Not only was there a possibility that she could remain childless forever, Tamar would also now be omitted from the share of tribal wealth that was indebted to her bloodline. *Goodness what heartbreak Tamar faced. Can we even blame her for what happened next?*

Tamar did what many of us do when we feel frightened and angry; she took matters into her own hands. Disguising herself as a prostitute she waited by the city gate to tempt her own father-in-law into having sex. It worked. She became pregnant with twins. When her father-in-law confirmed the twins were really his, he threatened to kill Tamar by fire, but God let her live.

Incest, immorality, prostitution, lies, potential murder, and evil schemes highlight the pages of this Holy book! Are you just as shocked as I am?

We have to stop and pause for a moment to consider this isn't just any family this is Judah, the son of Jacob and Rebecca. <u>Judah was the grandson of Abraham</u> and a descendant of God's *royal* family.

All through the Bible, God refers to Himself as, "The God of Abraham, Isaac and Jacob," emphasizing the significance of this hand-picked family. And this generational covenant was so much more than just a repetition of names to be recorded and echoed forever, it was a seal of blessing bestowed upon Abraham and his descendants.

Honestly, if I were God and had all authority, *which He does,* I think I would have wiped this story completely out of the Book, or at least filtered it. You know, cleaned the story up a bit to hide the scandalous sins and only reveal the safe parts. Seems more logical than to jeopardize the reputation of your chosen people. Am I right?

Yet, God never intended to whitewash the story. God intentionally kept these *REAL*, unfiltered details in His Holy Word because He wanted us to remember forever and ever. . .that He forgives mess ups and messed-up people. Those who others would easily disqualify, He handpicks, and invites them to participate with Him. He isn't just God to the perfect; the ones who win well, perform well, and live well - He is God to the rest of us, too!

This part of Tamar's story is when I realized God is so much more than I ever hoped for. Before I tell you about it, let's get *real*. If given the chance to recount our own family history, Tamar is the family member most of us wouldn't mention! You know it's true. We'd probably skip right over her, and hope nobody would ask how she's doing. Yet God displays non-biased grace when He deliberately includes her name in the historical recording and genealogy of Jesus Christ. *Often referred to as The Christmas Story!* It is here within these intentionally constructed sentences, God highlights Tamar! Wait, what? Yes! Read it for yourself:

This is the written story of the family line of Jesus the Messiah.
He is the son of David. He is also the son of Abraham.
Abraham was the father of Isaac.
Isaac was the father of <u>Jacob</u>.
Jacob was the father of Judah and his brothers. **Judah the father of Perez and Zerah <u>whose mother was Tamar</u>** (Matthew 1:1-3 NIV).

THERE SHE IS! No other woman has yet to be mentioned in the genealogy of Jesus Christ. Tamar is the first, followed by only four other women. Goodness gracious that makes my heart burst with overwhelming joy! If that doesn't put a new song of freedom and deliverance in your heart, then you need to read it again until it does.

There is absolutely no denying that God wanted us to never forget Tamar. Tamar the PROSTITUTE; ineligible by so many but still loved and handpicked by God! What a calculated cost our Savior made to include her here in His historical lineage. Introducing Tamar with some of the very best, God publicly validated her significance and kept her in the spotlight of His redemptive story!

Oh what a Savior!

God's ways rarely make sense to the world. He still chooses sinners like you and I, to showcase His story of redemption. His grace still protects and it commands, *those without sin can cast the first stone (John 8:7)!* It was offensive to the religious people then, and it still offends today.

Grace, this undeserved gift that can't be earned or purchased. The high value of its worth can never be altered by human hands. And God doesn't dispense grace with an eyedropper, He pours it out like the Niagara Falls making sure we can't miss it. When embraced, this extravagant gift has the potential to change every part of your life.

This gift of grace publicly declares You are worthy! You're not disqualified. Regardless of the negative labels others have tried to assign to you, or even the ones you've given to yourself, God still handpicks you to participate in His redemptive story. Besides, people rarely relate to perfection; when they see you haven't skipped through life untouched by heartbreak, sin, and struggle, they will invite you in. When you get invited, the opportunity for eternal rewards will be yours as you share your story of redemption.

So go ahead, I dare you to live *REAL*. Your unfiltered testimony, like Tamar's, displays unexplainable grace that will show others God intentionally makes room for all of us in *His* story!

Scripture Memorization
For it is by grace you have been saved, through faith—and this is not from yourselves, it is the gift of God—not by works, so that no one can boast (Ephesians 2:8-9 NIV).

Reflection
Grace. The five lettered word we often relate to as a word for *blessing* our food. That's a good thing, but grace is so much more than a spoken prayers! *Amazing* grace, which saved me from my sin and rescued me from its penalty, is the reason why I had to finish my assignment and publish this book.

You don't know this, but I delayed the publication of this book for over a decade. To be honest, I feared I had nothing notable to give. Really, what could my words create that didn't already exist? How could the personal, unfiltered experiences of my life make a difference to you? Still, a voice kept challenging my disbelief. That voice came in email form, posts on social media from people I didn't even know, and conversations of affirmation from the people I love. They all had the same message, "Have you considered writing a book? If not, you should." Let me pause and say, "thank you" so much for the encouragement. You pushed me forward and your kindness has been my motivation to reach the goal. Yet, I would be misguiding you if I only told you that part of the story. The *real* story goes something like this: **I failed tenth grade English**. *There, I said it and I feel better!*

I don't get commas, semi colons, or pronouns. I never have. I still use fragmented sentences and often times write too much like I talk. Believe me, I've presented my excuses to God a thousand times listing all the reasons I am not qualified to publish a book. I've even been known to use Moses' same excuse in Exodus 4 when he said, "Pardon your servant, Lord. I have never been eloquent, neither in the past nor since you have spoken to your servant. I am slow of speech and tongue." God wouldn't let me ignore Him. He kept pursuing me until He convinced me that a person's *real* life is so much more relatable than the perfect life they may want to trade it for. I am finally okay with the unfiltered, less than perfect version, because God instructed me to publish this book with redemption in mind.

Have you ever felt unworthy, or disqualified in some area of your life? Like me, you've probably lived with the tension between what others have convinced you to believe you deserve, and what God says you deserve. Can I tell you, these limitations will only keep you feeling guilty, unwanted, and unworthy. I am here to finish off that lie. You are worthy! Yes, you are. Let me repeat that on a new line in this book so it jumps off the page.

Help it to jump off the page, Lord!

YOU ARE WORTHY!

If no one told you this week, this year, this decade or ever, I'm yelling it as loud as I can. You are absolutely worthy of belonging, so believe it! You may have a history of people not letting you back in, but God will, every single time! To hell with every demonic and sinister voice that made you believe you don't belong.

To the girls who were raped physically or emotionally and grew up to hate themselves—<u>You are worthy</u>! I wrote this book for you. To the women who were abused emotionally, and now you believe the lie that you have to earn love. God wants you to know—<u>You are loved</u>! I published this book to reach women who have felt the undeserving sting of rejection, in whatever form it rolled up on you. Dry your eyes, stand up straight and go find your crown! Put it back on your head because you are royalty (1 Peter 2:9). When your Father is King, yes my dear, you are royalty. The world's attempts to disqualify you are futile when you have been called. <u>You belong</u>!

If this book is in your hands, God wants you to know: <u>You are worthy</u>, <u>You are loved</u>, and <u>You belong</u>! He has a better future for you than you could plan yourself. Let Him love You, just the way you are.

My prayer for you: Oh good and gracious God, thank you for Your love and Your amazing grace that transforms lives. I pray every word on the pages to follow, come in agreement with Your authority to bring healing and freedom to the broken and bound. Bind up the emotional wounds that are invisible, and heal souls that have mourned for far too long. Pour upon them Your oil of gladness, and with loving kindness make the broken whole again. I declare every negative voice that has tried to murder her potential be chased away, back to the pit of hell where it originated. Free those incarcerated by words that threatened her self-worth and identity. Embrace her with Your providential protection, preventing any lie from penetrating Your boundary. Freedom and deliverance is released as she enters into a relationship with You; a covenant that can never be broken. I pray women rise from the ash pile sent to burn them. Out of the embers they will take their rightful place in Your Kingdom, no matter the visible scars they bear. This day will be a catalyst for restoration and redemption. She will become an oak of righteousness, strengthened through struggle, a mighty warrior who will live to glorify Your name. Forever and ever, let it be - Amen!

#LetsGetReal
Thank God we don't have to look like what we've been through. - Polly

#2
BRUISED BUT NOT BROKEN

What doesn't kill you makes you stronger. - Kelly Clarkson

I am an imperfect girl, in an imperfect world, surrounded by imperfect people, but I was rescued by a perfect God. His love has changed my life and His mercy restored my past and His promises for my future are worth pursuing. But my journey hasn't always been easy. Like many, I've lived through some traumatic experiences and faced difficult people who I know were sent by the enemy, with the intentions to destroy my self worth and identity. For a long time I thought I deserved this deal in life. I stayed hostage to my pain and brokenness. This vicious cycle of defeat became even stronger when I let myself stay trapped in the opinions of others who branded my heart with their disapproval. Believing and rehearsing the lies of the enemy kept me in bondage to past memories I wanted and needed to forget. I lived hopeless and fearful I'd be stuck in "this season" forever.

Freedom came knocking on my door one summer weekend, during a conference I attended. The speaker, unknown to many, broke down in tears as she shared with us her *REAL* story. A story of abuse, enduring both physical and sexual abuse from her older step-brother, and giving up her child (the child of incest) at age fourteen. Her life, as she stated, was a big mess of dreadful memories until she found Jesus! She stood center stage. The light pushed brightly through the stained glass windows, illuminating the right side of her face, almost in a heavenly spotlight . . . **Unveiling her soul before us; she was frightened, but we felt free. She was broken, but we felt healed!** I had no idea that a college girl, with a fragmented life and a trembling voice, would change my life forever.

There were other guest speakers there who were all known; they had books and speaking opportunities, ministries and a following. This sweet girl, she had <u>His grace</u> and <u>His love</u>. She embraced it and it showed. Our lives became better because of her brave story.

None of us have it all together. We can attempt to hide the pain behind choice labels and educational titles, but behind closed doors there are some horrible scenes, unresolved conflicts, and complicated situations. We've all been broken and hurt until we hid. **Hidden things never heal well, though.** Like a wound covered by a bandage, eventually it must be exposed to receive proper healing. For many it can be hard to reveal your ugly story. You've been made to feel you don't deserve to heal. You've learned to suppress your feelings to protect yourself from those who were not safe enough to receive them. Healing requires feeling. You heal when you feel the anger, fear and injustice of your trauma. I beg you, don't be stubborn. They didn't know how to help you, but you still need help. Find a safe place for your heart to be unveiled and healed. But first, run to the Father!

In the middle of the pain you didn't cause, the secret reality you have to live with, be brave on purpose and run to the Father! **While you are embracing Him, He will be erasing the trauma that has suffocated your hope.** He will bind up your broken heart and bandage your wounds with His loving kindness. Your story doesn't need to be silenced, and the very parts of your life you wish to try and conceal, when exposed to the Healer, will heal.

You may have to live with a few scars, but let them be an everlasting reminder that the warfare you endured was not sent to kill you, it was meant to mark you with strength. Your "marks" bear witness to your mandate! You've been marked for greatness. *Oh yes you have.* **You carry God's seal of refinement on your life. Those scars are a holy branding that can't be bought or traded, and have been selectively given to those who endure. An eternal reward awaits the persecuted who still overcome (Matthew 5:12)!**

Dear sweet friend, own your scars! They are an eternal testimony that you survived what was intended to destroy you. God isn't finished with you and when others see your sorrow now wrapped in strength, it will allow them to believe that their scars can heal too.

Go ahead and tell your story, even if you're afraid and your voice shakes. Somebody needs to see and hear a Survivor point them to the life line of hope, and lead them to a safer way - THE WAY to Jesus!

Scripture Memorization
You intended to harm me, but God intended for good to accomplish what is now being done, the saving of many lives (Genesis 50:20 NIV).

Reflection
Each of us has an internal dialogue going on every day. In fact, you probably talk to yourself more than you talk to anyone else. You just don't say it out loud. *Well, maybe some of you do, LOL!*

Have you ever said,

I don't measure up.
I can't do this.
It will always be this way.
I'm too young or I'm too old.
God doesn't hear me.

Or maybe someone has said to you:
You ruined it.
You're pathetic.
I hate you.
You'll never change.
You don't have it in you.
You don't belong.

Words matter, every single one! We must understand the power of a word, because the words you hear, and the words you speak are prophesying to your future. Be careful to filter every word you speak. Allow only positive affirmations and life giving promises to come from your lips and hit your ears. You may suggest, I can do that, but you don't know the cursed words flying at me! *Yes I do.*

Make no mistake about it, there is absolutely a war on words! We all

have an enemy shouting words intended to snare us. His mission has always been to steal joy from your today and productivity from your tomorrow. He wants to detour you from everything God said you could have. You don't have to let him win. You just need to remind him what Jesus said. Start declaring the words written in red.

In Matthew 4:10 the enemy came to tempt Jesus with words to detour His future, Jesus said to him, "Away from me, Satan! It is written: 'Worship the Lord your God, and serve him only.'" When you counteract the lie with the promise of God, Satan will be defeated. The abusive words meant to harm you will have no power when they are strangled with the truth. His word never returns void (Isaiah 55:11)!

Nothing can be substituted for His words. You won't get to the place in God that you need to be until you learn to speak words that cultivate the future you desire. THE WORD OF GOD is the foundation for everything a *Believer* can become. His promises equal your potential, and believe me your potential is unlimited. Every word He declares you are, you should know! And every promise He said was yours, you should claim!

You may have endured hard things and difficult people that you believe have placed limits around you or stalled your progress, but be encouraged, every plot the enemy sent to harm you, God will use it to accomplish what He wants. Chaos and confusion may prioritize your thoughts about it, but can I tell you God can still produce an abundant harvest through barren times. He can still bring Heaven through your Hell.

God is not limited by obstacles, or enemies. The only thing that can stop the miracle is your unbelief!

Regardless of the circumstances that have been cycling in your family for generations, your words can put an end to every curse! We have the power to change the direction and course of our future. Genesis 50:20 became my favorite scripture verse over two decades ago. In unfair seasons I profess daily, "You intended to harm me, but God intended it for good to accomplish what is now being done, the saving of many lives." As I've reflected so many times on this promise, I better understand "the saving of many lives." My obedience, as does your obedience will affect the generations who follow. See your seed, your children and their children, won't have to face the same battles. The spirit of division, complacency, lack, pride, and duplicity no longer have to bleed in our bloodline 'cause we've fought and won some battles. We endured to overcome and now we have all authority to wave the white flag of victory in the devil's face and declare, "We own this territory, so get off of it!"

Today whatever you are facing down, declare Genesis 50:20. Fight the enemy with the weapon that will never fail, the Word of God. God will use this battle for your good and many lives will be spared because you prevailed.

Pray this . . .
Lord, I declare everything that has tried to work against me and mine, You will use for my good according to Romans 8:28. Every plot and scheme still in motion to keep me limited and fearful, is demolished. I don't have to listen to another lie the devil tries to conjure up. I will use the authority of Your Word, to abort His diabolical mission in my life and the lives that I love. There isn't a demon that has the ability to keep me out of what you have promised.

When I feel tempted to quit, and I struggle to believe my days will get better, bring hope through Your word, and strength through Your Holy Spirit. I invite Your Spirit to heal my hurt, and restore me to better. You have marked me for purpose! These scars I have, both hidden and visible will now be my reminder that I am an overcomer. I survived it! You're not finished with me yet. My greatest days are ahead. A new season of blessings are unfolding for me. I am confident my days are held in Your Sovereign hands - Amen.

#LetsGetReal
Your enemy may have given you his best hit on your worst day, but it still won't prosper. - Polly

#3
BECAUSE MY DADDY SAID SO

With faith you can move mountains and with doubt you will create them. - Author Unknown

There is a story in Luke 13 about a woman who was bound by an infirmity that was both painful and humiliating. For eighteen years she lived in constant torment; "She was bent over and in no way could raise herself up." She had heard about many miracles taking place, so Jesus became her ambition. Standing in a large crowd, Jesus saw her. He put His hands on her and commanded that she be set free. Immediately she straightened up and began to praise God. Not everybody was happy about it. The religious leaders were indignant that Jesus would heal a woman on the Sabbath. They rebuked *Him* and humiliated *her*. **With great compassion Jesus defended her, but more importantly, He identified her.** In Luke 13:16 He said, "This woman is a daughter of Abraham, whom satan hath bound." Interestingly, this woman's name is never mentioned. Jesus apparently didn't think it was important that His accusers know her name, but He made sure they knew she was a daughter of Abraham and belonged to the Father.

When you realize whose daughter you are, everything changes with your requests: the tone of your voice, your word choice, your posture and passion. **When you know who you are, you will approach Him boldly with confidence, and not as a cautious beggar. You will take your requests to the throne of God and leave them there, with no other back up plan. You won't waiver in disappointment because of delay. No, when you know who you are and whose you are, with your first breath you make the request, and with the second you will praise Him for His faithfulness to complete it.** When you really understand God's authority, the attempts of the enemy will no longer push you back to retreat, but they will cause you to identify with the Warrior who wins every time. You will bravely rise up and take dominion, declaring "Every place I step is blessed. Every area I occupy is blessed. My seed is blessed. My future is blessed because my Father said so!"

Don't let another tomorrow exist without believing you are a daughter of The King! You are chosen, redeemed for a purpose, and royalty runs through your blood. You are a seed of Abraham! Your spiritual inheritance far exceeds the stars in the sky. He delights in giving you the desires of your heart, so why then have you stopped asking? Why have you stopped believing?

In Matthew 21:22 Jesus said, "And in all things, <u>whatsoever ye shall ask</u> in prayer, <u>believing</u>, you shall <u>receive</u>." Your Father said you could ask in confidence. So ask and then live with unwavering expectation that He will do what He said.

I pray nothing the enemy conjures up today (or in your future) will have the power to intimidate you, detour you, or defeat you. Your Father has *all* authority and everything must rise and fall at His command. Take Him at His word; every one has promise. If He said it was yours, it's already yours. If your Father said you could, then you absolutely can!

<u>Scripture Memorization</u>
Yet to all who did receive Him, to those who believed in His name, He gave the right to become children of God (John 1:12 NIV).

<u>Reflection</u>
When my daughter Karson was about four years old, she was enrolled in the daycare program at church. At that time my husband was leading as the Associate Pastor with responsibilities to oversee the Daycare, the after-school program, and the School of Music. One day a teacher who meant so much to us, Miss Cindy, greeted me with a story about Karson. She said, "You will not believe what your girl did today." Karson was definitely one of a kind, (she still is) so nothing really surprised me. Miss Cindy told me on that day the daycare had a special practice in the worship center for their upcoming Thanksgiving program and they invited some of the parents and church staff to attend. Miss Cindy noted, "At the end of practice, Karson left the stage and started talking to some of the parents. You must already know she is turning into a social butterfly." I was thrilled to hear that Karson was so friendly, but I

already knew that. Miss Cindy continued, "When it was time to round the kids up for lunch, I motioned for them to get in line. Karson heard me, but continued chatting. Actually, she was ignoring my requests. When I waved to Karson, she waved back." Cindy started laughing and said, "With the loudest and most confident *Karson* voice I have ever heard, she said, '**My Daddy owns this place and he's the boss! His name is Pastor Torrey and He is my Father!**'"

We laughed until we couldn't laugh any more. I retell this story often because it's funny, but it also has significance. Karson understood that her Dad *was* the boss. On numerous occasions she watched him lead and give orders, take suggestions, fix problems, and discipline employees. Over the years she observed her teachers reach out to him when they needed assistance. Needless to say in Karson's mind, her father gave the orders, therefore He owned the place!

If we could face everyday with the same bold confidence knowing *My Daddy owns this place*, our lives would look so different.

I'm certain we would respond better to our problems. If you and I could grasp a similar child-like-faith, our confidence would never waiver when unexpected events seem out of control.

We wouldn't just limit our requests to only asking God to "bless our meals" and "give us a good night's sleep," we would ask Him to move mountains and then we'd watch them move!

We would walk into areas of chaos and demand it to cease!

We would lay our hands on the sick and declare supernatural healing!

We would occupy territory God said was ours!

We would curse demons, and they would flee!

We would declare the promises of God and live like we already have them!

We would speak life into dead areas and dead things, and watch God resurrect them!

Our conversations would change.
Our renewed confidence would swallow up fear.
Our misguided focus would shift from temporary things to prioritize the Kingdom; we would seek eternal rewards instead of earthly treasures.

If we really knew who our Father was, I believe our lives would look totally different!

Let me remind you, He is the King of Kings! He is a Shelter, a Refuge, and a Strong Tower. He not only speaks the waves into motion, but He can walk on them! The sun rises and sets at His command. When He speaks, angels obey. Where He walks, demons flee. He calls dead things to life. He reverses curses. Whatever He touches is restored to better. <u>Nothing is impossible for Him and there is absolutely nothing He won't do for you.</u> You are His! You are the seed of Abraham. He gave you a new name and secured your place in eternity. He promised everywhere you step you have dominion and authority.

Now go and live like it . . . because *Your Father said so!*

Pray this . . .
I am not alone. I am not abandoned. My Heavenly Father is active in my life. I prophesy to my future that no weapon formed against me shall prosper. Demonic assignments sent to me and mine are dismantled forever, by the power of The Holy Spirit. The favor of my Father surrounds me like a shield and opportunities will find me. Open doors will be granted. I declare increase in my life: increased strength, wisdom, discernment, favor and anointing. Things are shifting; there is a reversal happening. What was once hard, and showed signs of resistance, is now easy and covered with His provision. My Father is

bringing to me treasures and opportunities that He has chosen for me to steward. He is going before me, making crooked paths straight. My Father tears down traps and snares sent to harm me. He rebukes the devourer and my storehouse will overflow. My Father crowns me with His approval and He gives me dominion to occupy for His glory. Every promise He said was mine, I'm coming for! I am My Father's and He is absolutely mine - Amen!

#LetsGetReal
When unbelief tries to threaten your future, you can still confess the promise . . . "Because My Father said so!" - Polly

#4
JESUS HAD CRITICS

You don't have to keep explaining yourself to people who are committed to misunderstanding you. - Bishop Kevin Wallace

Perseverance and courage are necessary attributes to be able to stand for what you believe. Especially today, when everybody feels the pressure to *please* others. Many are afraid to speak the truth, and live the truth for fear they may be criticized or condemned. Our allegiance has been compromised, our attention detoured, and just like that - we've become more concerned with pleasing people instead of pleasing God!

These days, your obedience to God will absolutely tick some people off, and your steadfast commitment will agitate the uncommitted. Criticism is common for the Christian and if you're not enduring criticism, you probably are not much of a threat to the enemy.

Jesus had critics, lots of them!

He was extra controversial, yet He never allowed His critics to detour Him from His mission. On the night He went to pray, Jesus warned the disciples they would all turn away (Matthew 14:27). He knew when the assignment required obedience unto death, He would continue alone and the agony of broken commitments overwhelmed Him with sorrow. He started the journey with a full tribe. Everyone was engaged when He was walking on water, healing blind people, and multiplying happy meals; those were the good old days! But as soon as the disciples saw visible signs of rejection and controversy, they unfriended Jesus. At the first sign of resistance they stopped associating with Him and when their lives were threatened, everyone of them disappeared.

Jesus was criticized, rejected, and left alone!

How then can we expect anything different? No where in the scripture does it say that we will live void of critics. If the world criticized Jesus, they will criticize you. If they left Jesus, they will leave you. Jesus warned us in John 15:18, "If the world hates you, keep in mind that it hated Me first."

What all of us could use right now is a big, fat dose of bravery to persevere through the heavy assignments that will attract both private and public attacks. I get it, no one wants to be criticized, but trying to avoid criticism forfeits the greater purpose: God's plan!

Mary never asked to carry the Holy One, but it had to happen. God hand-picked Mary to birth the Messiah through a virgin womb. She endured unjust criticism from outsiders who knew nothing about her assignment. Threats were set against her mission, and it forced her and Joseph to flee for their lives! **Mary did nothing wrong. As a matter of fact, she did everything right!**

It's nice to have community support, and there's nothing wrong with desiring approval but sometimes what God asks of you will not be understood by others. Just the opposite may happen. You may have to face harsh critics and sometimes contend with those who rally crowds to abort it. Like Mary, you may have to leave all you know to protect your assignment from hostile environments, and with very little help. Are you willing to walk it out in front of your critics and naysayers? Are you committed to finish even if you have to finish alone?

Recently I read a quote by one of my favorite pastors. Bishop TD Jakes said, **"Your future victory depends on the criticism you choose to ignore."** *I felt that, did you?*

I decided a long time ago, I will not let a lack of support from others influence my commitment to finish, and neither should you! If God asks me to build a wall, slay the giant, construct an ark, fight an army or hang a Haman, I will obey!

Never forget that destiny calls one, but affects many.

Scripture Memorization

Blessed is the one who perseveres under trial because, having stood the test, that person will receive the crown of life that the Lord has promised to those who love Him (James 1:12 NIV).

Reflection

Jesus said in John 14:15, "If you love Me, you will <u>keep</u> My commands." Obedience to God matters. And maybe we aren't obeying Christ because our love for Him has been overshadowed by our pursuit to find love in the world. Have you gotten off track? Are you living your life more concerned about keeping happy those who continually misunderstand you? **It's possible their reactions reflect they have no idea the weight of the assignment you carry!**

Nehemiah had a crucial assignment to build a wall. He was attacked repeatedly by those who felt threatened by His progress. Even so, Nehemiah stayed committed. With a sword to fight in one hand and a plow to build in the other, Nehemiah honored the Lord. He faithfully built the wall.

Noah was criticized for obeying God's instruction to build an Ark. Noah's generation had forgotten about God. They were corrupt and violent so God decided to destroy the earth with a flood. Noah's critics were aggressive in their attempts to ruin his reputation, but he didn't detour from God's instructions. For more than one-hundred years Noah looked foolish until it started to rain! Thank God for Noah's tenacity to persevere through the criticism. His decision to finish the assignment literally saved our lives!

Deborah, one of the most influential women of the Bible is known for her courage to persevere. She was a worshipping warrior. Deborah was more brave than her male colleagues, and God appointed her to lead an army of men to victory over their Canaanite oppressors! Deborah was publicly criticized for being outspoken and confident, but she didn't let it stop her from completing the assignment. She finished victoriously.

Mary the mother of Jesus received public criticism that threatened her life, and her seed. She still remained faithful. She gave birth to our Messiah, and defeated the enemy with the arrival of His authority. Thank God Mary ignored the slander and false accusations. Her obedience opened her womb to house the Divine. She overcame the adversity to birth our King, the Savior of the world.

You and I should be careful to consider what we criticize. We could be speaking against the assignments and purposes of God! <u>Shame on us!</u>

In a cynical culture growing rapidly with harsh criticism, God is looking for the remnant without excuse, who will rise up and declare, "Here am I Lord, you can still send me!" Bold, tenacious, audacious, obedient women that can handle loosing the love of the world, to embrace the love of the Father.

I want to be found faithful, no matter the cost. What about you?

My prayer for you: *(Whether your current assignment is to raise kids who love and honor the Lord, start a missionary work, teach, preach, build a ministry, serve the homeless, etc. they are all important to God. Obey, commit and finish well.)*

I heard the Lord say, there is a season of conquests ahead of you, but first He must deliver you from the weariness and soul-sick discouragement you've carried for seasons! I speak deliverance over your life. Be free from pleasing man! In your last season, dishonor and rejection came from people you loved but they never loved you back! Critical voices, tainted with jealousy tried to kill your potential and almost diverted you from the mission, but no more - in Jesus name. God is bringing immediate closure to attachments with hidden motives. Destiny thieves who fought to keep you out of your assignment are falling away and will disappear. He will illuminate the wrong voices that seek to misalign you and they will flee like chaff in the wind. What this last season of discouragement stripped from you, God said you didn't need for the future.

No doubt your assignment is heavy, but everything needed to finish, is already in you! **Go ahead and visualize the promise again. Recite it! Rehearse it! Believe it, because every thing you have seen in the Spirit, shall come to pass**. As it is in Heaven, so shall it be on earth! Go boldly in the name of the Lord and accomplish your assignment. You can not fail, for He surrounds you on all sides - Amen.

#LetsGetReal
People think if they don't support you that will hold you back. If need be, God will put total strangers in your path to support your assignment. - Polly

#5
WAIT IT OUT

Jumping to conclusions won't get you there any faster. While you're trying to figure it out, God has already worked it out. - Polly Herrin

You can tell a lot about a person when they've been denied access. Rerouted by GPS because of a construction zone, skipped over at the DMV line, or put on a long hold by a telemarketer can get to even the best of us. My unfiltered moment usually happens when I can't remember one of my five-hundred-seventy-three passwords and I'm denied access. I am quick to lose my patience every time. I usually mumble and grumble loudly and whatever is closest to my reach gets slammed; like the nearest coffee cup, book, or kid. *I'm just kidding.*

None of us want to be denied access; we don't like to wait. We've been groomed by society for quick fixes. The day we live in you can buy a car on the internet and have it shipped right to your home in twenty-four hours. Friends, you can even have a mini facelift, while adding twelve inches of hair, all during your lunch break. They call those "extensions" by the way, just in case some of our male friends are reading this book with us. *LOL!* We are spoiled Americans, receiving what we want, when we want it. So it's no surprise when we expect God to work just as quickly. I mean come on, He's God. He created the whole world in six days, so why can't He provide the solution to our need in less than a day? Wisdom warns, God's Kingdom doesn't work in our ways and our timing. Isaiah explains to us our waiting has benefits and promises to bring renewed strength and power (Isaiah 40:29-30).

God never presses pause out of spite. If He makes you wait it's always for a purpose.

Hannah, a woman well acquainted with waiting, can be read about in the book of Samuel. Hannah was extremely loved by her husband. The bible tells us she had a double portion of his affection, yet Hannah's heart still grieved in sorrow because she did not have a child. She had an unmet expectation and the hope of ever becoming a mom looked impossible. To make matters worse, Hannah shared her husband with a woman named Peninnah. This woman was "fertile myrtle" and gave birth to many children. We might presume Peninnah would be sympathetic towards Hannah because she was barren, but she was just the opposite. The Bible described Peninnah as Hannah's rival: malice, vindictive and insulting. In today's terms we would 'straight up' call Peninnah, a bully.

There is nothing worse than sharing space with a vindictive woman who has the evidence of blessings, while you are still barren. *Can I get an amen?*

Every day Hannah endured the taunting of Peninnah. Every day she and her tribe of children pranced around the campsite while Hannah looked at her two empty arms void of children. Hannah's maternal clock was ticking and her days to conceive were numbered. She was desperate, heartbroken, and for years she felt forgotten.

How many of us have felt the desperation of a closed womb, a closed door, a closed heart, or a closed mind? Oh the agony one endures when day after day we live with unmet expectations, knowing God could meet them, but He hasn't. But before we linger too long in hopelessness we must pause for a moment to consider the facts in this story, and ask an important question: **Who closed up Hannah's womb? The Bible tell us in first Samuel 1:6, "The Lord closed up Hannah's womb."** To acknowledge this fact is an important detail. God, the giver of life, who had every ability to open her womb, was more than able to grant Hannah's request for a child. God had a plan, despite what it looked like to Hannah. He was strategically orchestrating the exact time when He would open her womb and Hannah would give birth to her firstborn son, Samuel.

Don't miss this! Samuel would become a prophet, chosen by God, to anoint Israel's next King who happened to be the shepherd boy we all know as David. Scholars believe David was between the age of 10-12 years old when Samuel called him from the fields to publicly anoint

David as Israel's future King. If Samuel had been born a few years earlier he may have died before David was ever born, missing his moment to anoint him. You see God strategically orchestrated every part of Samuel's story, especially the exact timing of his birth, because he needed Samuel to fulfill a purpose greater than himself.

Timing is crucial to your destiny too! The seasons you are made to wait have strategic purpose. God is not pushing you off or ignoring your requests - He's not disengaged or inactive. He is working on your behalf. Even right now, He is aligning people and events to facilitate His purpose. Your heartache is about to turn into hope.

It's *His* story - let Him write it. I assure you, it will all make sense soon.

Scripture Memorization
For my thoughts are not your thoughts, neither are your ways my ways, declares the Lord. As the heavens are higher than the earth, so are My ways higher than your ways and My thoughts higher than your thoughts (Isaiah 55:8-9 NIV).

Reflection
Waiting on God's plan to unfold is potentially one of the most sanctifying aspects of the Christian life. We all have to wait, and when we don't see the answer right away, we can feel as if we are the victim of God's unfairness. To heighten the pain of your wait, the enemy wastes no time trying to convince you God has not heard your prayers. He threatens, *This is it. This is how it will always be. Nothing will ever change for you.* I beg to differ! This seemingly delayed season has significant purpose, and your unmet expectations are just a starting place for God to do so much more than you ever dreamed.

Hannah had to die to her preconceived ideas. She had to give up control and release some things, so God could do His best work.

Give up your idea of how it's going to happen. When the world is chanting, "Just do it!" God says, "Just wait on it!" The answer isn't in what you can do, the answer is fully attached to what God will do. Trust

God. Turn your focus back on His unchanging character, and abandon all preconceived ideas of how and when it should happen. You can be fully confident that His plan is much better than the one you've been working on!

Pray this . . .
Father, I don't know what the future holds, but I know You hold my future. When I am afraid, I will trust You (Psalms 56:3)! When I am downcast and distraught, I will put my hope in You (Psalm 42:5)! When I am eager to rush ahead, help me to understand the benefits that come when I wait (Psalm 27:14)! I ask for the strength and willpower needed to endure this long season of intense frustration. Force my hands off of situations You want me to leave in Your care. When the enemy attacks my mind with doubt and fear, and tempts me to take matters into my own hands, raise up a standard against him. Disrupt his schemes to detour me from Your Sovereign plan. I declare this waiting season has significant purpose that will bring great benefits to me and mine.

I will walk by faith and I will wait in faith, so help me God - Amen.

#LetsGetReal
Let Peninnah laugh today, very soon your son will anoint kings and hers will serve them. - Polly

#6
YES, MY GOD WILL!

Faith isn't just knowing God can, it's believing He will. - Polly Herrin

The story of the three Hebrew boys, Shadrach, Meshach and Abednego, is one that brings me incredible hope and exuberant peace in the midst of hard circumstances. Let's dig in a little. While King Nebuchadnezzar was in reign, he erected a ninety foot tall golden image and demanded everyone bow down to his god to pray. He warned the Babylonian people that if they didn't bow, they would take their last breaths in a fiery furnace. Not everyone was on board with the king's demand; Shadrach, Meshach and Abednego were committed to worshiping the one true living God and refused to bow to this false god. King Neb was angered by their denial of his requests, so he sent messengers to arrest the boys. Still they remained committed to their God, and with the famous three words **"We will not bow,"** they were escorted into the furnace before the crowd.

They said,
> King Nebuchadnezzar, we do not need to defend ourselves before you in this matter. If we are thrown into the blazing furnace, the God we serve is able to deliver us from it, and He will deliver us from Your Majesty's hand. <u>But even if </u>He does not, we want you to know, Your Majesty, that we will not serve your gods or worship the image of gold you have set up (Daniel 3:16-18, ESV).

I am certain hell was celebrating at the sight of revenge, while King Nebuchadnezzar had a front row seat. His arrogance was heightened as he declared his public victory, but only for a *hot* minute! *Ha! I had to throw that in there.*

No other king, not even Nebuchadnezzar, had a chance against <u>THE KING!</u>

King Neb's victory dance was cut short when he was shocked to see not only three men in the fire, but four, and the fourth One was confirmed as "the Son of God!" God showed up. He always does.

God is looking for brave, faith confident people to partner with Him to do the impossible. Their hope is not confused or easily deferred in threatening situations. People who walk by faith are unmoved by the enemy's threats and they never bow down when the Truth is challenged. They rise up in the face of adversity, with an *even if* attitude and declare "My God will show up!"

Do you have an *even if* attitude to stand against the culture who wants to turn lies into truth? When the fire is turned up to test the validity of your faith, can you stand alone when everyone else bows?

Your conversations will quickly prove who you are in times of uncertainty. As the enemy sends a threat to your family, your finances, your freedom, or your future, what comes out of your mouth determines what you believe about God. Every single one of your conversations should reflect that your God will never fail! It's time for the enemy to hear faith in your words.

Declare by faith:

Even if I don't see a way, God will make a way.
Even if the provision seems impossible, my God will provide.
Even if the dream seems out of reach, my God will make a way.
Even if I am not yet healed, I won't bow down to fear.
Even if I am criticized, I will still finish my assignment.
Even if the world bows to lies, I will stand for the truth.
Even if...(you fill in the blank)_____, I won't bow down!

God is drawn to extravagant faith. Start verbalizing His abilities in your struggle and watch miracles unfold. Don't quit because there is always more to the story than your survival. The Hebrew trio saw a miracle that not only changed their lives, but also the life of the King. The fiery furnace was intended as a weapon of destruction, but ultimately God used it as a miracle of transformation. King Nebuchadnezzar ended up acknowledging Jehovah as His God. That's exactly why the enemy fights so hard against your speech. He knows your testimony to God's faithfulness will always draw others to our King.

Courage is contagious.

Today, somebody is hoping and praying you do not bow in defeat! They are watching your faith on display and so much depends on the choices you make to stay standing or take a knee. The children you raise, the neighbor you barely know, the co-worker who doesn't believe yet, they are watching and listening! Don't you dare bow down in doubt. Your provision could come tomorrow! Your deliverance may be in the next breath of praise you sacrifice, and that miracle you've been waiting on, you may see it before sunrise! *Oh I believe it.*

Keep believing that God will do what He promised! Your life is going to be a witness to the grandness and greatness of our King. Yes, My God will . . . He will absolutely make a way!

Scripture Memorization
Now to Him who is able to do exceedingly abundantly above all that we ask or imagine, according to His power that is at work within us, to Him be glory in the church by Christ Jesus to all generations, for ever and ever (Ephesians 3:20-21 NIV).

Reflection
Martha and Mary were the sisters of Jesus' best friend, Lazarus. They begged the Healer to come and save their brother, but Jesus delayed His visit and didn't arrive in time before the sisters pronounced him dead. Three days later, *count them one, two, three* - Jesus showed up and commanded Lazarus to get up out of that grave. Lazarus immediately shed those grave clothes and walked out of the tomb. So believe it when I tell you, there was a reason Jesus used Lazarus' name to call for him. **If Jesus had only said, "Come forth," every single dead thing in that graveyard would have gotten up and walked out because that's the God I serve!** How am I so confident? I have

experienced His miracles, extravagant miracles only God could provide. I saw Him heal the hole in my son's heart and the surgery cancelled **Praise Break!** I witnessed God eradicate my husband's $66,000 educational debt with the generosity of two people in a month's time. **That's My God!** One September afternoon in Tampa Florida, God's hand of protection shielded me on Interstate I-4 when I was involved in an accident with five other vehicles. Two individuals were transported by air to local hospitals, and two were driven by ambulance, but I drove myself home! *I can't stop now. . .* God showed up for my sweet girl Karson. Her hope was to go to a specific Christian college with no desire to apply to other schools, even though this college was the most expensive on her short list. *If you know Karson you know, she was never going to settle.* Karson believe God would somehow show up on her behalf and that's exactly what He did. Even when it looked impossible, God made a way. Karson's extravagant faith got the attention of God, and He provided a scholarship that paid all four years tuition. **Yes He did - that's the God I serve.** My friend Brenda was diagnosed with breast cancer. She embraced that "even if" faith. She woke up every morning telling the enemy, "Even if the scans still show cancer, I'm not bowing in unbelief. It is well with my soul." Today my friend is cancer free! **Oh, Yes MY GOD WILL!**

It's one thing to know God can, but another to be able to declare, "Yes He will!"

Nothing is impossible for our God! Nothing! Sometimes we have to remind ourselves of the miracles He has already provided, so we can live in expectation for what's to come. Let me encourage those who may be struggling with unbelief. God is able and willing to change your circumstances. He is no respecter of persons so don't let the enemy convince you otherwise. It's possible God's slow response is a purposed delay, in order to grow your faith! **Your faith is the soil for the miracle on the way; the kind of miracle that leads you to walk away saying, "Only God could have done this!"** You see, I'm learning extravagant faith is dependent upon a God-experience. If you never needed healing, how would you know He was Jehovah Rapha? If you'd never been lost in sin, how would you understand Him as the Good

Shepherd? A need or an impossible situation that can't be fixed in your own strength, always puts you in the best place to experience Him as Jehovah Jireh! The fiery furnace moment you are fighting so hard to escape, could be a set up for God to show up.

Make this difficult season a "Holy place" where you fight through the unbelief. Tack back your confidence and believe God. Then, live with expectation He will show up, and the results will unfold into your greatest place of victory. Don't you dare quit!

Pray this . . .
Lord, I don't understand this consuming fire that surrounds me. My faith has often faltered. This delay has convinced me You were no longer working on my behalf and I have bowed to uncertainty and unbelief. Forgive me! No more wavering faith. Instead I will believe Your Word. These limitations I see are the exact place where Your miracle can begin. I resist the temptation to doubt Your promise, and even in this fire, I will partner with You. The flames will not burn me but only remove what has restricted me. I will not bow. I will remain steadfast until the promise arrives. Amen!

#LetsGetReal
God can <u>not</u> take what the enemy meant for evil and turn it for your good, if you give up in the middle! - Polly

#7
BETTER TOGETHER

You don't have to stop loving people just because they stopped loving you. - Polly Herrin

Penguins, those cute, chunky, black and white birds, can survive in forty below zero weather with winds up to 120 mph. They've learned the benefit of "huddling" together by making a circle formation; they squeeze in as tightly as they can, penguin skin to penguin skin. Ornithologists *(that's a person who studies birds, in case you were clueless like me)* say the center of the circle can reach temperatures as high as 72 degrees Fahrenheit. Despite how miserably uncomfortable the huddle can be, the penguin remains because their survival is completely dependent on their connectivity!

Today, loneliness and isolation is a real thing for many. People have stopped huddling, and really who could blame them. Are you one of them? I'm sure you have good reasons to avoid people who've been careless with your heart, so I can't hold it against you one bit. But what we often fail to realize is our escape to fly solo is not only in opposition to God's plan, but it also makes us visible and vulnerable to the enemy. Doing life alone makes you a sitting duck, and an easy target to destroy. *No pun intended.*

God created us to connect with one another. The phrase "one another" is derived from the Greek word *allelon*. It occurs almost one-hundred times in the New Testament alone and over fifty of those occurrences are specific commands teaching us how to (and how not to) relate to one another. Love one another, encourage one another, comfort one another. You get the idea!

God designed relationships and according to Ecclesiastes 4:9, you can be good by yourself, but you won't be great without connection to the right people.

National Geographic replays a video of a herd of antelope grazing on a hillside. I've only seen the video once, and that's more than enough for me. The videographer zooms in to feature one of the hungry deer moving away from the herd to an enticing patch of huckleberry. The foolish fawn knows it's a risk to go there alone, but his desire and aching stomach detours him outside of community. Within seconds he becomes dinner to the winter wolf. *Big sigh -*

Leaving community, especially spiritual community, makes you vulnerable in many ways. People will fail you. People will hurt you, but in comparison, the enemy is on a mission to destroy you. Satan isn't a little man dressed up in a red suit with horns who pops his head out to scare you. He is diabolical and evil! His mission is to attack everything God established, and the end goal is to divide and conquer. When you stay offended, you are playing right into his hands. When he sees you move way from the huddle, remaining isolated and vulnerable, he will quickly move in to ravage you to destruction. Don't let him win! Instead, forgive the offense and stay connected to community.

Psalm 133:1 says, "In unity there is a commanded blessing!" This is exactly the reason why the enemy fights so hard to keep people hurt and excommunicated from the group, because he doesn't want you blessed and he certainly doesn't want you protected.

Division never glorifies God. It weakens hearts, homes, communities, and the Kingdom. On the contrary, God promises there is supernatural strength in unity. One can send a thousand to flight but two will send ten-thousand (Deuteronomy 32:30). Our ability to fight off the enemy multiplies when we stay connected.

Find your tribe, and whatever it costs, fight for unity where the blessing will overflow.

Scripture Memorization
Two are better than one, because they have a good return for their labor: If either of them falls down, one can help the other up. But pity

anyone who falls and has no one to help them up. Also, if two lie down together, they will keep warm. But how can one keep warm alone? Though one may be overpowered, two can defend themselves. A cord of three strands is not quickly broken (Ecclesiastes 4:9-12 NIV).

Reflection
Who did you write off and who have you broken relationship with because they acted offensively? Let's get *real*; people hurt people! We <u>all</u> have the potential to hurt others. Don't be so self-righteous to think you haven't.

She hurt you, I hurt her, you hurt me. Please people, <u>we all got our feelings hurt</u>!

If you could walk one week in her shoes you'd see what she's been enduring, and you'd be less quick to "wish her dead" because she rubbed you wrong. She's faced warfare, and suffered through things most people can't even talk about; evil plotted against her by an enemy who wants to destroy the assignment she holds. She is weary. You keep saying, "she's hard to get a long with." Darn right she's hard because she had to survive warped people. She's a survivor and she doesn't trust anyone. **While you wrestled to get your jeans on this morning, she wrestled demonic principalities, and you're offended she didn't say hello first?** It was all she could do to dress herself and show up! None of this was even about you . . .

We should be very careful with people. We have no idea the battle they endured the day before, or the one they will wake up to tomorrow. Be kinder. Be gentle with souls seeping of sorrow. Chase down and fight for those on the verge of breaking community.

She may look tough, but she's so fragile. Give her the grace you have already received. When she crosses your path abruptly, or even offensively, realize God is giving you another opportunity to love her. Do it quickly and without needing to be validated first. Your willingness to embrace her, with undeserved kindness and perpetual patience could be the very thing God uses to reach into the darkest

places of her soul, and allow her to believe that God heard her prayer!

As women of God, we <u>must</u> expect to be positioned in tough places to love *first*, to selflessly look past the fault *first*, and to seek reconciliation *first*. Girl, nobody said it would be easy. Stop judging and start praying for tougher skin and a tender heart to better endure the hurts that sometimes come from huddling together with imperfect people!

Jesus extended to us the gift of grace before we ever deserved it. His crucifixion sealed that grace, and with every laceration on His back, He took our sin and freed us from its penalty. Forgiveness never comes without a cost, but He was always willing to pay it. No matter how many times we offend Jesus, He is ready to welcome us back to the circle. Shouldn't we be more like Him?

Pray this . . .
Lord, You warn that offenses will come, but enduring them is not easy! To be honest, it hurts to "turn the other cheek," especially when my face is getting warped by the same person! In my flesh I don't want to forgive, I want to push back. I wanna fight. I want to make them pay for the sleepless nights, and unproductive days their wrath has made me endure. I don't feel like forgiving them especially when they haven't sought it from me. They have taken so much . . . please Lord, heal my heart.

Forgive me when I have expected more from others than I have given. If there is anyone who has escaped my circle that I need to rescue and invite back in, give me the humility to do it. I will make it right. I want to live under Your commanded blessing. I want to be an initiator of love and help to cultivate community where others can belong and be strengthened. Give me a heart of understanding, words that bring healing, and arms that shelter and protect. Help me to love as You have loved me - Amen.

My prayer for you: God, I pray for the person reading this devotional who needs freedom from the traumatic experiences in her past. The ones that took her breath away and knocked the hope out of her life. She doesn't trust people, and how can we blame her? I pray You chase her down, and bring her back to a safe community. Let every fear be silenced. Deliver her from the schemes of the enemy that sought to keep her out. Bring alignment to her life through relationships that speak to her potential and send those who will be willing to embrace her to wholeness.

I also pray for the person who feels their experience isn't as traumatic, but who has still been hurt. It is not Your will that any of us be victims of wrongdoing. I pray she quickly forgives, starting with the ones who never asked. At the moment she opens her mouth to confess, step in without delay and do Your work. Holy Spirit, do what I cannot do with my human words or human hugs. Go deep into her soul and mend what's been broken, deliver what's been bound, restore what's been vandalized, rescue what's been stolen! In the name of Jesus we pray - Amen.

Personal Declaration
I am released from _____ *(state the name of the person(s) who offended you or the event that happened to you.)* That offense will no longer dictate my response to them or others. I reject every negative, untrue, hateful, unrighteous, demonic word ever spoken over me. I break those words off my future; they are powerless and have no life. Every evil, abusive, and unjust act violated against me, You will avenge, Lord. The memories of these brutal acts are diminishing, and the hold of those events will no longer define me. Heal every area that is still traumatized by the injustice. I declare healing in my body, mind, and soul. No longer will I sit passively by and let the enemy steal my purpose or my destiny. What he has already taken, he must bring back. I call back stolen territory, forfeited time, crippled hope, lost investments, estranged relationships, and compromised peace. Anything that was rightfully mine, must be returned. It shall be as if it was never stolen.

My future is secure in you. My identity is found in You! My purpose is sealed in You. I will do my best to overlook offenses and know that when I do, You will command a blessing with tangible evidence of Your favor. To the best of my ability I will forgive and live in unity with others. Let the words of my mouth, and the meditation of my heart, be acceptable in thy sight, O Lord, my strength, and my redeemer (Psalm 19:14 KJV) - Amen.

#LetsGetReal
Forgive people and start with the ones who never asked! - Polly

#8
GET UP GIRL AND SPEAK

God is not obligated to defend your words, but He is obligated to defend His. - Polly Herrin

Who harassed you, harmed you, or violated you so grossly that you no longer have a voice or a vision? Worn out and hopeless, you feel tempted to surrender because the thought of fighting another stinkin' day makes your body shake in turmoil. Sleep is no longer kind to your fragile soul, so you pop pills like tic-tacs and depend on liquid caffeine to function day-to-day. The enemy has taken so much from you, hijacking your thoughts and arresting your willpower. This warfare has left you emotionally disfigured and weak. Somehow he's convinced you to believe, it will always be this way. He is a liar, and before he attempts to finish you off, I beg you to remember who you are! You don't have to stay here in this place of destruction or abide in circumstances that ravage your soul. You have a choice.

A crisis is no time to prepare for victory, because we never think clearly in times of trauma. You must make up your mind now that you will focus on where you want to be, not where you came from. Focus on your healing, not the sickness. Focus on what remains, not what you lost! Focus on the promise, not the problem.

The fact is whatever you choose to focus on today, you give permission to exist tomorrow! And when you allow it to occupy your thoughts, that thing will grow. We will never win battles rehearsing the lies of the enemy, but we can use the authority of His Word to annihilate every forged attack!

Are you struggling? Do you feel weary and weak? Open your mouth and declare, "In my weakness, He is made strong." (2 Corinthians 12:9-10)

When the enemy threatens it's impossible, prophesy, "With man this is impossible, but with God nothing is impossible!" (Matthew 19:26)

When fear threatens your sickness and disease, you speak up and shout back, "By His stripes I am made completely whole." (Isaiah 53:5)

When you have a need, speak to it, "The Lord is my Shepherd, I shall <u>not</u> want."-(Psalm 23:1)

If your days are void of fulfillment and purpose, start declaring the promise, "I shall see the goodness of the Lord in the land of the living." (Psalm 27:13)

In bleak situations, when your emotions are spiraling out of control and you question if you will survive this next season, grab on to Romans 8:28 and decree it: "God is, and will, work this thing for my good!"

Open your mouth, fight with His sword and win with this promise because "Greater is He that is in me than he that is in the world." (I John 4:4 NIV)

You might have to live in today, but you can speak the promise to your tomorrow! His words have the substance to form new life, a new perspective, and new hope. His words, when spoken, shall pierce bone and marrow to heal the things you can't even talk about. That's who my God is and that's what He does!

Jesus said, "In this world you will have trouble, but take heart I have already overcome." This is your banner of victory. Stop letting the enemy silence your voice. This is your hour. This is your moment to speak up. Deliverance could be hinging on your decision.

Get up girl, and speak life!

<u>Scripture Memorization</u>
As it is written: "I have made you a father of many nations." He is our father in the sight of God, in whom he believed, the God who gives life to the dead and calls into being things that were not (Romans 4:17 NIV).

Reflection

If you don't know me personally, you may not know that I am an avid reader, student and prophesier of God's word. I don't say that to boast, please hear my heart. I share this to testify that without His promises and correction over my life, I would be one big mess!

When I first began to realize His words were life changing, I was in my late twenties. I know that's pathetic since I'd given my heart to the Lord at age eight. My parents did well to raise me by His words, and to teach me the value of His words. So you understand when I say I cringe with remorse thinking of all the years I wasted so ignorant of the power of scripture. There is no one to blame but myself. My lack of desire to read and study the Bible forfeited the revelation and empowerment it gives. When I finally sought out His words and embraced them for myself, these promises became my lifeline of survival and the prophecy of my future. It was exactly as David described in Psalm 34:8, "I tasted and it was so good!"

Everyday I mediated on His words, the more transformation took place and these benefits were immediate. The Word within me was transforming everything about me! I gained confidence. I had a new perspective on old problems. I received spiritual strength and fortitude. I rested better. My thoughts were in alignment with His will. I learned to love better. The bitterness I harbored in my heart for years, began to be chiseled away bit by bit. Fear and anxiety no longer handicapped my days. I felt empowered, like I'd never felt before.

I wanted my children to have this same opportunity and I began to teach His words to my kids. I even started a Moms group *(Moms On A Mission)* with the sole purpose of teaching and equipping our kids to be followers of Christ.

My husband and I began to require scripture memorization like we required our kids to complete homework assignments. Sounds super-spiritual, and to some outside observers, we looked radical and extreme. Yet, when we weighed the eternal consequences of teaching them how to set a table, throw a fast-pitch, or drive a car

versus teaching them God's promises, the Word won every time. There really is no comparison. . . only one has eternal rewards!

Together as a family, the first scripture verse we memorized was short, but packed with so much power. I intentionally chose Proverbs 6:2, "You are snared by the words of your mouth." At the time I had no idea the extreme impact this Proverb would have in our lives for decades.

As Noah and Karson matured and became teenagers, I would hear them share this scripture out-loud with confidence, rebuking any negative word spoken over them. Even today, if anyone from the family uses the word "can't" in a sentence, (*example: "I can't do this anymore!"*) Karson is swift to respond with, "You are snared by the words of your mouth," and quickly challenges us to instead declare, "I can't yet!'" (Oh the power of one word!) Our son Noah now uses this declaration almost everyday of the year on social media when he professes, "This will be the best day ever!" He's learned even if that day has the potential to be his worst day, he can do as Jesus did and call those things that are not, as though they could be (Romans 4:17 NIV). This behavior is not living in denial as some would suggest, it's biblical! Living by faith and activating your faith to believe God for the impossible is more than pleasing to God.

God's word has all authority, and when you speak the word it will not return void - it will always accomplish its purpose. Today is the day to stop living passively. Don't waste another day cursing your future with words like, "Things will never change," "I'll never own a home," "I'll always have to settle." No! No! No!

You have the authority with your mouth to speak life, and to reverse the curse! It's your choice. Poverty, lack, illness, abuse, chaos, and destructive cycles may have run in your family, until it ran into you. You are anointed to break that cycle!

Speak up Girl. Today it stops with you, because you will prophesy to your tomorrow and it will be different!

Pray this . . .
Lord, according to Your Word I shall overcome by the blood of the Lamb and the word of my testimony. I am an overcomer. Every thing I need to face off with my enemy, You have provided. His attacks are futile in comparison to Your authority. Even if it looks like it has always been this way, I take back my voice to agree with Your promise. The words of my mouth will testify to your goodness and bring life to my life and the lives I love.

From this day forward: I will mediate on your words. I will believe your promises. I will embrace them as *the* authority. I will use Your promises to prophecy to my future and the future of those I love. I will no longer live unintentionally, wasting my God-given days. With my words I will speak freedom to the bound, and hope to the hopeless! With expectation, I will live to fulfill all You have ordained for my life. Your purpose and plan shall prevail. I declare this in the name that is above every name, Jesus Christ of Nazareth - Amen.

Declaration
I am blessed.
I am living with purpose and I will fulfill God's plan for my life.
I am a leader, and not a follower. I walk in the anointing and favor of Christ. I live in the Shadow of His protection. I am healthy. My mind is alert and sound. My heart is strong. Every cell in my body is functioning as You created it to function. The organs in my body are string and healthy. Anything sick and broken is healed. I commit my body to the Lord and obey His commands to care for it well.
My future is blessed. My relationships are blessed.
My finances are blessed.
My seed and offspring is blessed.
I will gain influence and increase.
I will lend and not borrow.
I will store up financial blessings for the next generation.
I will lead and not follow.
I will take territory and occupy land.
I will increase and see overflow.
I will make wise decisions.

I will live in peace.
I will lack no good thing.
I will overcome every obstacle set against me.
I will see new seasons of growth.
I will be blessed with ideas that will bring financial rewards.
My finances will multiply.
My God dreams will live and not die.
My children will inherit these blessings.
My children will honor the Lord with their lives and with their lips.
I shall see the goodness of the Lord in the land of the
living and my house shall see His unending favor in tangible ways.
According to Deuteronomy 28:8
I am set above and God has commanded blessings on me. All that I touch shall prosper.

#LetsGetReal
You may have to live in today, but you can speak the promise to your tomorrow! - Polly

#9
UNHURRIED

When the time is right, I the Lord will make it happen. - Isaiah 60:22

I love the story of Esther who demonstrated the incredible power of a woman submitted to God's plans and purposes. Esther 2:12 describes in detail the process Esther had to comply with, before meeting the King. This was a big ordeal; a process she could not skip. Esther needed to learn the etiquette required of a young woman before addressing a royal parliament. It was necessary she be submerged in the culture to adjust, according to their way of life. It couldn't be easy. I'm sure Esther questioned the tedious and long process, but she still willingly endured. Her obedience to God proceeded her elevation, when she would stand before King Xerxes to make a bold request that would save her life, and an entire nation. In God's Kingdom, preparation precedes purpose.

For a few years I was employed in central Florida as an educator. Occasionally I would see a student seated in the hallway with their belongings, and usually it was because they showed up unprepared. The hallway gave the student a place of solitude, where they could gather their thoughts, work on the problem or finish the assignment required. Although to the student this "time out" seemed like punishment, it was really an act of grace! The same is true when God makes you wait, it's always for your good. Maybe you're not ready for what's next. Experienced, but not mature enough. Talented, but not humble. Wise, but not brave enough to face your critics. Extremely gifted, but horrible with money. To you it may seem unfair, but really this season of waiting is covered in grace.

When my daughter was about eight years old she was grounded to her room. She wasn't enduring the "time out" as she should. From down stairs her father and I could hear her stomping on the floor, slamming the bedroom door, and continuing to shout rude sentiments to her brother. My sanity was being provoked! I walked upstairs, opened the door to Karson's room and gave my final warning, **"Karson, if you keep**

acting like this I promise, you will remain in this bedroom until tomorrow morning - no dinner and no play time. I have heard enough. <u>Now, you can wait pretty or you can wait ugly, but you are still going to wait!</u>"

This hard season of parenting made me exhausted. I took a seat on the edge of the stairs, and there I uttered a silent prayer asking God to help me understand this child. In the same way Jesus addressed Martha when she was complaining about Mary, I felt God say, "Oh Polly, Polly, Polly! You need to heed your own advice. You certainly have your moments when you don't wait pretty either." Friend, I literally laughed out-loud. Certainly not in disrespect, more like - You got me God. It's down right embarrassing to admit those outbursts of childlike frenzies didn't just happen as an eight year old, more like a forty-eight year old. Looking up to Heaven I had no choice but to nod in agreement and confess, "Lord, please forgive me for the many times I did not wait pretty."

God is unhurried and still doing His greatest work in you. Surrender your timeline in favor of His peace, and recognize this waiting season is a gift you will never get back. Use it well, because what you prepare for today, will matter most tomorrow.

You're not forgotten, you are anointed and next in line! Your day in the palace is quickly approaching - I pray you will be more than ready for it.

Scripture Memorization
Let perseverance finish its work so that you may be mature and complete, not lacking anything (James 1:4 NIV).

Reflection
Remember when the iPhone introduced us to a new feature called SIRI? SIRI is the male or female voice that functions to help you navigate hands-free. Years ago, when I first heard about SIRI, I was ecstatic because I knew this voice dictation feature would save me a ton of time. I can be impatient at times, okay a lot. I'll admit I rarely take the time to review my text messages that sometimes showcase

grammatical errors and misspelled words. I usually do my best editing after I hit send. *LOL! Shame on me! My family and close friends are hysterically laughing right now because they've all gotten at least one of my corrupted texts they had to decipher.*

So you can imagine my excitement to try out this new SIRI function that promised quicker and more efficient ways to complete tasks. One day, a text came in from my mother. Again in a hurry, I decided to try this Siri function. I clicked and held down the microphone icon, and recorded my response back to my Mom. I felt so accomplished and using SIRI was easier than I thought. I was convinced this new feature would work for me.

Later in the day I had a chance to follow up and when I saw Mom's response I was confused. In all caps she sent this message back to me: **WHAT?!** Then Mom used the little emoji with a "pointed finger upward," directing me to look above. Oh no, my Mom never uses capitalization, exclamation points or emojis! I knew something was terribly wrong. I scrolled back up on my phone to review the message I sent to my Mom, and I couldn't believe my mistake.

I thought I said:

"Thanks Mom, love you lots."

But SIRI heard and dictated:

"Thanks Mom, love ya slut!"

What in the world? What have I done! **<u>Who calls their mom a slut?</u>** Sorry again Mom, I love you, but honestly it has made the best sermon illustration ever.

When in a hurry and rushing ahead, we have the potential to make huge mistakes, and much bigger mistakes than calling your mom a slut!

Demanding our own way will never hurry up God. There are no shortcuts to divine destiny. Those who skip out and try to find the shortcut will wind up being, cut short. Waiting on Him is a beautiful surrender; a Holy participation that has many rewards.

Embrace the wait! He will do more for you in your waiting than you could do in your striving. It's never wasted time when God makes you wait.

My prayer for you: Lord, we all struggle with waiting. I pray the woman reading this devotional knows that You heard the prayer, you are fully aware of the request. You are not disengaged nor are You inactive. You have the best plan ahead. The heaviness and weariness of the weight has taken a toll on the way she is doing life. Hopelessness has set in and she feels stuck. I pray your Holy Spirit comfort her on a different level. Restore hope to her hurting heart. May she be fully aware that You will keep your promise. Give patience and long-suffering to those who need it. This world is filled with noise and unrest. It seems as if society has exchanged busyness for productiveness, and we are easily tempted to do the same. Slow us down. Let us get in rhythm with Your heartbeat. Forgive us for the times we rushed ahead. It only proved we didn't trust You. We don't want to settle for our plans, we want Your will don in our lives. I declare You are completing a good finished work for my Friend. Every dream, desire, and promise, is Yours to fulfill. **Let her be confident that she doesn't need to "work it" but instead she can walk with You to accomplish it!** Amen.

#LetsGetReal
You can wait pretty, or you can wait ugly, but you're still gonna wait! - Polly

#10
TELL THE DEVIL, "I'VE CHANGED MY MIND!"

Rest well, knowing God is in the business of undoing whatever the enemy tried to start. - Polly Herrin

How many times have you felt handicapped by overwhelming circumstances? All of us have lived through despondent seasons when it seemed like we'd never escape; times when reality looked nothing like the promise, and you questioned if God would stay faithful. *Yes, He will!* It goes against the very character of God to be unfaithful. Although at times it may seem He is absent, there is nothing you are going through that isn't under His jurisdiction and authority. There's not a demon in the underworld that He can't get His hand on. There's not a witch throwing out a hex He can't eradicate! There's no chain on your life that He can't break. That dead thing, He can still resurrect!

God's not just Sovereign one day, He is Sovereign all of your days! And no matter the impossible situation you find yourself in today, God can still undo whatever the enemy tried to start.

Daniel was thrown in the lion's den . . . BUT GOD!
Jarius's daughter was on her sick bed . . . BUT GOD!
Baby Moses was left in a basket on the river surrounded by crocodiles
 . . . BUT GOD!
Paul and Silas sat in prison wrongfully convicted . . . BUT GOD!
Joseph was hated by his brothers and left for dead . . . BUT GOD!
Joshua faced a wall . . . BUT GOD!
The Israelites faced the Red Sea . . . BUT GOD!
David faced a giant . . . BUT GOD!

The ultimate victory came when Jesus was buried and left for dead. His mother mourned, His disciples fled, and His followers were shocked with unbelief! Crucified and hanging from a cross, it looked nothing like He promised. Imagine the despair looming in the air that day as they pulled Jesus' lifeless body from the cross, and buried Him in a borrowed grave. How could the Kingdom come to earth if the King was now dead? On that evil night when all of hell celebrated, and it looked like satan had the final blow, God's truth still prevailed!

Jesus, was the Son of God and His followers remembered Jesus once made a promise, that if the temple was destroyed, in three days He would raise it up again (John 2:18-19). *Praise God!* Raising Himself up from the tomb, He victoriously walked out conquering death, hell, and the grave. Jesus kept that promise and you can be assured, He will keep the rest of them.

You see, the facts of your situation may say one thing, but God's truth will always override the facts!

Hard times, when endured, have the potential to produce miracles that will always point to God's faithfulness. God will never fail, so hold on to Him when you feel like all hell is strategizing against you. Stop and declare, "The facts I see today may look different than the promise, but I expect a *"BUT GOD"* moment to happen soon."

Scripture Memorization
Then Jesus came to them and said, "All authority in Heaven and on Earth has been given to Me (Matthew 28:18 NIV)!"

Reflection
Brave, strong, confident women are often misunderstood - all the brave, strong and confident women said, "Amen!" Most brave women I know have been through something to give them that identifiable strength that fosters qualities of persistence and endurance. The common denominator of a Survivor: they endured something. Survivors endure things that are often hard to articulate but regardless if she speaks about it or stays silent, her strength is visible in the way she fights her battles. Unless you've walked through the same experiences it may be difficult to relate to the intensity of her warfare.

There have been many unseen battles that were sent to destroy her that you know nothing about. So please, stop judging women for being brave and strong!

I remember one night laying on the floor broken, weak and weary, begging God to give an answer to my question, "Why this again?" He quickly reminded me the enemy was after my tomorrow and all the promises ahead. And then I felt like God said, "Get up! Go find your sword (The Word of God) and use it!" The next part may shock some of you, but I don't need to explain God. I never heard God audibly, some people do, but I felt God said, "If you don't fight it, your children will have to!" I knew exactly what the "it" was and "it" scared the *hell* out of me.

Excuse my language! I needed to emphasize it the way I felt it that day. Hell is a real place ya' know. I didn't send anyone to hell with my words, I'm just describing my emotions. So let's move on.

I remember telling God I didn't want to face another battle. I asked Him if He could give it to somebody else. He said, "Polly, this time you are waring for your assignment and your peace! When this victory is won, you will pass the deed of ownership down to your children and their children. Never again will this *beast* occupy your territory. It will be defeated forever."

When I heard God say that my children were in jeopardy, my entire perspective changed about the battle. I felt a force of energized determination, and a Holy Spirit confidence pick me up off the floor. <u>I became a Mom on a mission.</u> I heeded my marching orders and went straight to my home office, grabbed my Bible, and fanned the pages until it landed on the book of Titus. I sought wisdom, stayed in prayer, and fasted. Honestly, I never realized what this battle would require of me, decades of unrelenting warfare. I'm not here to seek sympathy from anybody, only God knows the details of the warfare I've endured.

I'm a Survivor, that's exactly why I KNOW I have been commissioned by God to speak with authority, and confidence to those still surviving. I had to survive *it* to free generations that would follow! Not all who came before me survived *it* and I saw *it* take life from them. My bible ensures that whatever we overcome, the generations who follow won't have to fight (2 Kings 10:30). That was absolutely enough for me to stay engage. I was determined to survive it.

You can't let your feelings dictate your decision. You can't sit passively on the sidelines wishing the enemy would disappear or change his mind. There can be no negotiating with the enemy, because he's too cunning (Genesis 3:1). You resist him! Tell him to flee back to the pit of Hell from where he came! Use your weapons (the Word of God), and open your mouth to pray. Every victory will be undeniably linked to prayer and prophesying of the Word of God. A life marked by prayer is a life marked for miracles! Warriors assigned to break the spells of Hell have to live in continued prayer. They understand the enemy can never penetrate through the power of the name of Jesus! Don't be mistaken, it's never my words or your words that bring victory, but the power is in His words, the One we pray to! As a Child of God, you have been given all authority and a straight line of access to the Name above every other name. Satan will be defeated when you tap into your sacred rights. Prayer is your spiritual right! Use it! Keep petitioning God to move on your behalf. Pray in the Spirit. Pray the promises. Pursue His power and then repeat!

God said the effectual and fervent *prayers* of the righteous avails much (James 5:16)! The accurate meaning of that word *prayer* here means supplication. It means to pray with a burden, until something happens. *Read that last sentence again, please.* When was the last time you lingered in fervent prayer? Not just leaned over a cup of coffee with your notebook in hand and wrote out your prayer, filling in the pages with colors and artistic expression. Certainly there is a time and a place for that type of praying, but when you are in warfare and fighting to survive, you need to pray and fast with intensity!

Pray until something breaks! Pray until the enemy resigns!

God is calling warrior women who know how to travail in Zion. Women who know how to call to Heaven with fervent prayers and supplication. Attaching themselves to the authority of Jesus Christ and then storming the gates of Hell to take back everything the enemy has stolen. The consistency and fervency of your prayer life will give you the spiritual stamina you need to fight with passion until you see the victory!

You may only have faith the size of a mustard seed, but you can still use it.

Do not give the devil the satisfaction of your silence. Open your mouth and tell the devil, "I've changed my mind! I'm not believing a word you say! Regardless of how this circumstance appears, and how long you've held me hostage, I believe my 'BUT GOD' moment is on the way! I will see a victory."

Personal Declaration
Satan, the blood of Jesus is against you! Nothing you can conjure up has authority over me. God is my Way-maker, my stream in the desert, my Defender, and my Rock in sinking sand. You will protect me when I am awake, and while I sleep. Any person or event sent to divert me, hurt me, or detour me from God's assignment, must submit to Your authority. The Mighty Warrior will deal justly with my enemies. God will chase down and smite every single one. This mountain that I keep circling, I will circle no more. God will move this mountain or He will carry me up it. His resurrection power is alive and working within me. This is my season to prosper! This is my season to overcome! This is my season to possess all that God has put my name on.

My prayer for you:
I pray every trap set up against you by the enemy, be destroyed completely. Every attempt of manipulation to block you from God's purpose, be dismantled. What others have said about you, done to you, or may even be planning now against you, will have no authority over your assignment or your peace. I pray you heal from things no one ever apologized for. Be free from harsh words and evil deeds. *Yes, Lord do it*

now. Free from the hurt, the event, the act! I pray you're free from anxious, fearful, and tormenting thoughts. I speak peace to your heart and mind. You will walk in the way of the Lord, knowing the weapon may be formed but it will <u>never</u> prosper (Isaiah 54:17). God will bless your going in and coming out. You have been assigned to overcome, and you will overcome. Right now, God is undoing what the enemy started. He is pushing back the darkness. He is strangling the very enemy who tried to strangle you. The Kingdom of God cannot be shaken, and every enemy is defeated, by the authority of Jesus Christ - Amen.

#LetsGetReal
The thing that you defeat easily is never the real battle. The real battle is what keeps coming back to test the validity of your faith.
- Polly

#11
LOVE EMPOWERS, JEALOUSY DEVOURS

Pay close attention to those who don't clap when you win! - T.D. Jakes

This is for the women who tear down, talk down, speak down, and look down at others. Mean women, who isolate and intimidate with closed circles, closed hearts and closed fists. Tell me, why is it that women more than men, are jealous of another's beauty, talent, or calling, and are you one of them? Secretly despising another woman for her beauty, the shape of her body, the amount in her paycheck, or the opportunities that gravitate to her, is unpleasing to God.

One of the verses God used to show me how dangerous jealousy can be is found in James 3:16 which says, "Where there is jealousy and selfish ambitions there is <u>every type of evil</u>." A jealous heart gives open access to every evil spirit. My goodness, if we would just take heed to that warning and understand the consequences we would turn from envy. King Saul is an example of what happens when jealous thoughts fester. Saul started comparing what the people said to him, versus what they were saying about David. He was overtaken with jealousy and wanted revenge. Saul's unrestrained actions caused him to loose honor with the people and not long after, He took his own life.

Jealousy left unchecked will grow and devour everything in its path.

Comparison is an unhealthy scale that always lie! We are not souls to measured, we were created for relationship; to be embraced. It's difficult to embrace someone you envy. Turns out that gifted and favored woman of God, whom you despise secretly, the one you try to rally your friends against, she could be the very gift God sent to comfort you, to protect you, or possibly promote you! Stop resenting people who have more talent, more influence, and opportunities. God can give you the same blessings and you don't have to violate another woman to get it.

David prayed an incredible prayer in Psalm 51:10-11 (KJV), "Create in me a clean heart, O God and renew a right sprit within me. Cast me not away from thy presence; and take not thy Holy Spirit from me." King David wasn't perfect. He too had his dirty little secrets. He committed adultery with Bathsheba, and plotted to have Uriah killed but He was always willing to allow God to fix his heart. He quickly confessed his sins and God took notice. God can't operate in deception, or denial but He will absolutely transform you with truth. **Thank God that He still confronts what we ignore and will reveal what we are much too willing to hide, because He desires for us to be free.** Are you jealous? Do you secretly despise another women? If anyone came to your mind lay aside this book right now, and ask God to forgive you. I pray you heed His call, and repent. Don't carry those spirits into your future another day - be free!

Let's break the chains of jealousy by refusing to act like adolescent girls, warring and scaring one another from our own insecurities. Instead we can intentionally show up to celebrate one another, out-loud and on purpose.

I'm cheering you on. I promise, I've got my pompoms in my hands, I'm raising them high and shouting your name because you deserve to shine!

Scripture Memorization
A heart at peace gives life to the body, but envy rots the bones (Proverbs 14:30 NIV).

Reflection
I've been on both sides of the thin-blurred line of comparison and jealousy. I'm not proud about it, I'm just being *real*. Yet, I too have been on the receiving end of jealousy, and have deep scars to prove it. It's not worth it. Oh I pray God makes you brave to flee from circles that tolerate slandering tongues, and I pray you resist belonging to environments that don't applaud others when they win. You don't belong there! You belong to the One who created you to fulfill an incredible purpose that has significance to outlive you, so believe it!

Let's be the one:
- who roots for the other girl, the one we don't even know.
- who encourages a total stranger, because words bring life.
- who believes in others, even before we have someone believe in us.
- who includes instead of excludes.
- who praises publicly when she feels like she's failing privately.
- who forgives first.
- willing to turn the other cheek, no matter how much it hurts.
- who extends kindness without anticipating any in return.
- who loves without motives.
- willing to give second, third, and fourth chances to those who still fail us.

Jealousy never propels one toward the plan of God, but instead opens doors for evil and chaos to have access in your life. When you don't repent, this spirit will continue to take residency in your bloodline. You will raise jealous girls and your sons will marry them! Be obedient to God's calling and repent. Your freedom and the freedom of your bloodline depend on it.

Together we can do so much more than anything we try to do on our own. We need you, but we can't have you in our circle with a jealous heart. We need you whole and healed!

Pray this . . .
Dear Lord, I've been jealous of _____.
Forgive me. At times my lips have been slanderous, and my motives impure. Forgive me and redeem my lost soul. When I am hurt and feel the need to ruin another with my words, let me find my worth in Your words. When I feel most tempted to despise another for her beauty, talent, promotion or opportunities, remind me of my significance. You have good plans for me, to prosper me in all my ways (Jeremiah 29:11). I fully embrace my unique gifts no matter how different they look for hers and instead of being tempted to focus on her talents, teach me how to seek You to develop mine.

Let my words be uplifting and encouraging. May my hands reach out to embrace the unloved. Give me opportunities to extend an invite to those who feel uninvited. Let love radiate brightly through my deeds, and use my words to fill the empty parts of her soul with kindness. May she feel so loved and accepted in my presence that she knows she belongs. I'm ready to be that girl. Amen!

#LetsGetReal
People who talk bad about you with hopes that others won't find you so appealing are jealous and insecure. Regardless, still talk good about them. - Polly

#12

DREAM AGAIN

If Heaven started it, hell can't stop it. - Polly Herrin

Joseph had a dream and shared it with his brothers. Doing so almost cost him his life. *(Let's pause and think about that lesson for awhile!)* Joseph was noticeably favored by His Father, and he often bragged about being the favorite. Extremely jealous about it, his brothers plotted against him, and took steps to make sure Joseph never came back home. It's much easier to accept unwanted consequences brought on by the poor decisions you made, but when you find yourself detoured because of others' ill intentions it can be hard to believe that God is still in control. From a pit to a jail cell, Joseph's life was marked with obstacles completely out of his control.

Esther's story is one like Joseph's. She was orphaned at an early age, and raised by her Uncle. Unbelievable odds were stacked against both, Joseph and Esther. They lived the majority of their lives fighting to survive, but if you've ever read the ending to these stories you know one obtained authority, and the other became a queen! Strangely though, nowhere in the book of Esther is God ever mentioned. Yet so descriptive in evidence, His handprint was orchestrating every day of Esther's life. God was always with her and He is with you! Whether it seems He is or not. Whether He speaks, or if He remains silent, He is absolutely still in control of this difficult chapter filled with impossible people and prolonged problems.

He is still writing your story, and no matter what, hell can never stop what Heaven starts!

You may feel lost in process. You may even struggle to believe you could ever get back on track. Can I encourage you in this hard season that maybe the obstacle is part of the transition. Maybe what you consider a set back is a strategic set up to prepare you for something greater.

Every transitional moment that looked like it was detouring Joseph was actually developing him to become an incredible leader that would highlight him for promotion. He was detoured far away from home, yet he was exactly where he was suppose to be. He was falsely accused and landed in prison, but God kept him captive for his protection and promoted him in the presence of his enemies. The ride to the top will often include a visit to the bottom, but it's never without purpose. Eventually these unexpected series of events Joseph endured led him to Egypt where he earned the trust of Potipher, the King's Commander. Joseph was elevated to second in command, placing him in the exact position that his original dream foreshadowed. **Look at God!**

Sometimes the process you go through looks nothing like you dreamed or imagined. You can easily be deceived by what you see in the natural that you loose sight of the eternal. **Refocus! You're not lost, you are in transition.** This journey is absolutely the place that you will not only discover your abilities, but you will also discover your Source. These *hell-like* experiences are the place you will see who He really is, Jehovah God. These troubles don't hide Him; they actually will reveal Him and His purpose. Keep trusting God no matter how far detoured you seem from the dream.

God's destination for Joseph was always the palace and His plan involved more than what Joseph imagined. What if Joseph gave up and quit on his dream? Do you realize an entire nation would have perished by famine. The nation of Israel lives today because one man continued to believe the dream. You may feel like you've been forgotten and unable to reach the finish line but this season is only temporary so don't unpack your bags. Your steps have been ordered by the Lord and the *dream* is still in the plan. Whatever Heaven starts God will finish!

Scripture Memorization
The steps of a good man are ordered by the LORD, And He delights in his way (Psalm 37:23 NKJV).

Reflection

Joshua and Caleb were the descendants of God's people who were promised to occupy land, sworn to their forefathers. Along with ten other spies these men were sent by Moses to survey the land. The ten came back with a negative report that compared themselves to grasshoppers in the site of giants. With that comparison they nullified in their minds what God promised would happen. **Unbelief always disrupts God's plan!** Sadly those ten spies, plus others who remained in unbelief, never entered the land God said they owned! Only Joshua and Caleb believed God and occupied the territory.

This story gets me every time! What a tragedy. God told them the land belonged to them, all they had to do was go and possess it. For decades they wandered in the wilderness, journeying just outside the borders of the land they already owned, but never living in it because they couldn't believe for it! Can you relate to journeying so close to the promise but limited because of unbelief? You're not alone It seems its hardest to stay optimistic when there is no tangible evidence in any way, to validate what He promised.

The ten spies made the mistake of looking at their opposition through natural eyes. They had a vision problem and kept seeing their obstacles as bigger than their God. Unless we are able to see God correctly, it will never look possible!

The ten talked as if they needed to take the land in their own strength, Joshua and Caleb insisted they could take the land in God's strength. There is a difference! Please take the pressure off yourself and be at peace knowing whatever you commit to God, He makes prosper (Proverbs 16:3). It is the Dream-Giver's delight to bring about the ending from the beginning. You don't have to know every detail, because He already does. He is orchestrating events to prosper you. He is assigning the right people to support you. When you are able to live day to day confidently knowing what is for you won't miss you, you'll never turn back. It's freedom like none other.

It's really easy to assume we've missed it, when we see others are living the dream and we are still wandering and wishing in the dessert. Your journey may have landed you in a parched place and it looks like you will never be able to escape. Getting back on track may feel out of reach but the truth is: **You can't miss it unless you resist it. Just keep believing.** Unbelief will threaten every promise God said was yours.

You deserve all God has for you and I pray you get it. But you won't get it until you believe you can have it. Make the choice as Joshua and Caleb did, and decide you are well able to take the land. Give yourself the freedom to believe in the dream again. It is absolutely within your reach and nobody can answer that purpose like you!

Personal Declaration
I shall finish every God ordained assignment. Every obstacle I face, every plot planned against me, every impossible situation is preparing me for the next place I will occupy. Elevation will proceed my adversity because My God is faithful to keep His word. I am determined to hold on to the dream(s) God gave me regardless the resistance I may face. When God intends for something to happen for me, it shall not delay! I will not quit. With God's help, I am well able to take the land - Amen.

Pray this . . .
God, increase my faith! Let my vision see past the natural into the supernatural realm. You are the God of the impossible with unlimited miracles and resources. I know You must think it simple, the things I daily ask You for, and my request can be so so finite in comparison to what You can do. You are unstoppable and victorious. No longer will I be a slave to fear or confined to the dreams only living in my heart; they shall be birthed and they will transfer from generation to generation. You will make a way - Amen.

#LetsGetReal
Stop surrounding yourself with ten who say it's impossible! Find the two who believe you are more than able to take the land.
Let's go! - Polly

#13
WHEN GOD SAYS NO!

God's "no" is just as holy as His "yes"! - Polly Herrin

Most of us are elated and filled with outbursts of gratitude when God immediately opens a door for us, which in our finite minds translates to a resounding "yes". It's not so easy to respond in the same way when God remains silent and seems to be inactive. Closed doors can feel offensive in every way because they deny access, but in God's Kingdom, even His "no" is as beneficial to you as His "yes".

Have you ever considered that maybe God's "no" is for your protection? Maybe He is keeping the door intentionally closed, because He sees areas that are unpleasing, and if exposed would keep others from giving you the respect you deserve. Behind the closed door is a moment, or we could say a gift of grace, where God can correct, restore, and develop you privately. He's not keeping you locked behind the door because He's mad at you or finished with you. My Friend, behind the closed door He is doing His best work in you!

When leaving home for an extended stay we take great precaution, and do our due diligence to make sure every door is locked. Locked doors keep intruders out! Many have added security systems they will activate, and some even go a step farther turning on inside and outside cameras to monitor activity. Why? To keep thieves from stealing stuff!

Anything valuable is vulnerable to the thief.

You are valuable to God! What's inside of you is a huge threat to the enemy. You've got gifts, talents, and dreams that with the correct development will be used to train and equip others. There are opportunities in your future that are bigger than you can imagine. Your life shows evidence of potential fruit, that God sees needs to be protected! Just maybe God has locked that door to deny someone access to you. He saw the ill motives, He heard the conversations when you weren't around. That person may have looked like a "pot of gold", but God saw beyond the surface of things and blocked entry! *That's a good place to Praise God!*

Not everybody deserves access to you . . .

When the enemy realizes he can't take you down from the outside, his next play is to position somebody who can destroy you from within. For Jesus that was Judas. If Jesus had an inside enemy, you probably have a Judas too. Bishop TD Jakes identifies Judas with one sentence. "Judas gives an ear to your critics!"

You thought it was your fault the relationship ended but the truth is God put an end to it. See, all this time you've been assuming God is being unfair, but really He is defending and protecting what is His. God will mess up your plans, before they mess up you. Get use to closed doors!

Don't you override His authority, and chase down what He removes. Rejoice in His "no" as much as you rejoice when He says "yes"! Wait on God to bring the right people, the right opportunities, in the right time. Give Him thanks right now, for the many times He has already detoured the enemy from having access to you.

Scripture Memorization
But those who wait on the Lord shall renew their strength; They shall mount up with wings like eagles, they shall run and not be weary, they shall walk and not faint (Isaiah 40:31 NKJV).

Reflection
In today's culture, lingering, waiting, and enduring the process seems like a lost discipline. This generation looks for quicker ways to the same result, but most of the time great things take time.

Have you ever seen someone take a drink of coffee and say, "Oh those beans are good!" Probably not. Most likely you've never heard someone suggest, "The hot water in this coffee is delicious!" We say things like, "This java is bomb" or "This coffee is delicious." Really it is a collective cooperation of the elements that work together <u>over time</u>, to make something good. It's a process! Most definitely in my cup of coffee, it's the peppermint mocha that makes it better.

In Romans 8:28 God promises He works "all things for your good." He didn't say just some things, He said <u>all</u> of them: every closed door. difficult season, and difficult person. Every person that left, the one that stayed, and everyone that's coming, has precise purpose in the shaping of your future. You may not be able to understand it right now, but even in your heart break, God is working. You may be tempted to question, what stays, what leaves and what slips away, but in Christ Jesus, <u>it will ALL work together for your good!</u>

God didn't orchestrate every step of your life to this point, and then decide to leave the destiny of your future solely in your own hands. He is in control; working even when you can't see it or feel it.

While you are waiting, don't waste the days. Put your faith into action. Faith is more than giving thanks, faith means we praise Him before the deliverance comes, before the answer, before we see the provision. You don't have to understand to fully embrace this season. Just trust that when He says, "no" it is always because He loves you.

Pray this . . .
Lord, help me to love Your "no", as much as I love Your "yes". Forgive me for the times I've doubted what You were doing. Forgive me when I acted selfishly and took matters into my own hands. I know it was unpleasing to you. Only by Your Spirit can I stay joyful, when my heart feels hopeless. As I stand here in front of this closed door that feels like rejection, I still will trust You. If it's blocked and locked, I accept it as evidence of Your protection. I will refuse to weep over what You have blocked. I refused to mourn over what You removed. I refuse to resurrect what you have cursed.

I ask You for wisdom as I pursue God centered relationships! Bring Kingdom connections into my life. Those who will partner with me on the same mission, to bring honor and glory to You.

My desire is to be a vessel You are pleased with. Mold me, remake me if you have to, I want to be used greatly by you - Amen!

#LetsGetReal
Thieves never go to empty vaults, they seek loaded vaults filled with potential and promise. - Polly

#14
JUST REMEMBER

The enemy hates your potential. The real fight isn't over where you are, it's over where you're going - Polly Herrin

Do you feel desperate, overlooked, anxious, worried, forgotten or defeated? Well, take a note of this, **"What you feel is not always real."** I love that quote, and I wish I knew who originally penned it so I could adequately give credit to the truth behind those words.

The enemy is good at using our emotions and feelings to obscure our perspective. God may seem hidden, distant, removed and voiceless to you. Others claim they know God's will and you feel bewildered. Others feel victorious and you feel forgotten. Regardless of what you are going through this very day, you do not need to give in or give up because no matter what you feel, God is continuously in control. He not only spoke the universe into being but He governs it with His authority. You need to remember who God said He was, not who You see Him as.

He declared He is:

> Jehovah Elshaddai, the Lord God Almighty.
> Jehovah, El Elyon, the Most High God.
> Jehovah Adonai, our Lord and Master.
> Jehovah Yahweh, He is Lord.
> Jehovah Nissi, the Lord our banner who protects and defends.
> Jehovah Raah, He is our Shepherd.
> Jehovah Rapha, the Lord who heals.
> Jehovah Shammah, the Lord who is present.
> Jehovah Tsidkenu, our God of Righteousness.
> Jehovah Mekoddishkem, The Lord who sanctifies.
> Jehovah El Olam, He is everlasting.
> Jehovah Elohim, He is God by Himself.

Jehovah Jireh, the Lord who provides.
Jehovah Shalom, He is our peace.
Jehovah Savaoth, the Lord of Hosts.
Jehovah Roi, the God who sees.
Jehovah Gmolah, the Lord of recompense.

He is God from before time until everlasting. He is the God of the impossible and there is nothing He can not do! With only His words, He spoke light into existence. He created all of creation. The stars, the galaxy, and the planets are on our God's resume! From dust particles He formed mankind. Look around and take notice of the amazing earth you call home. His handprint is everywhere! The majestic mountains and flowing rivers showcase His astounding work. Watch how the ocean stops at the borders He imposed and observe the waves that still billow to land because of His authority. Never have the sun and moon stopped rising and setting at His command. My goodness, if we would open our eyes we would see the greatness of our God. He is absolutely outstanding - unmatched in every way.

Is there anything too hard for Jehovah? Absolutely not!

Even as creation echoes His glory, and angels in Heaven bow before Him, our unmatched God, longs for you. **He longs for you!** The God of infinite power and might, The Holy One, whose name presides over every other name, desires a relationship with you. He proved it, when He sent His only Son to the cross to suffer the worst kind of crucifixion, so we could have eternal life. And just so it's clear, God asks nothing from you except that you believe.

Many have distorted the way to God. You don't get God because you have it all together, or because you earned a Master's Degree in Theology. You don't have special access to God because you are intelligent and can understand His ways. You don't even get God because you do good deeds like feeding the hungry, clothing the poor or sheltering the orphans. Being a "good person" and doing "good deeds" isn't the requirement needed. **You get God when you believe!**

You believe Jesus is the Son of God and that He died for your sins so you could have everlasting life (John 3:16). Once you receive His forgiveness, He promises you will be in covenant with Him for eternity.

Our amazing God, <u>the great I AM</u>, is as close as a whisper. Whatever you need Him to be, He already is.

<u>Scripture Memorization</u>
God is not a man, that He should lie, nor a son of man, that He should change His mind. Does He speak and then not act? Does He promise and not fulfill (Numbers 23:19 NIV)!

<u>Reflection</u>
Mercy and grace have followed hard after me, chasing me down with songs of deliverance! Covering my shame and promoting me in spite of my imperfections and failures. I will forever be thankful for the love of God that has no boundaries or limitations. I don't want to minimize His mercy and grace that made a way for me to escape my penalty.

But . . . it has <u>always</u> been His words that smitten me!

I've lived through some experiences where God's Word was the only love left standing. I walked through frightening times when all tangible support was leveled to the ground, and His Word became my shelter. In the weight of anguish and heartbreak that threatened my future, God's Word gave me an unexplainable hope to still expect better was coming. When I thought I couldn't go on, His promises told me I definitely could. His words pierced through bone and marrow to bring emotional healing I could find no where else. In dark places when evil surrounded me, His words protected me, and escorted me from the fortress of dysfunction, leading me to paths of safety.

Standing at my father's death bed watching him struggle to take every breath, because of the cruel disease of Dementia, God's Word comforted me: "Though I walk through the valley of the shadow of death, I shall fear no evil, for God art with me (Psalm 23:4)." I knew God was with my Daddy.

In my challenging seasons of motherhood, with all the mistakes and unknowns, I can be confident that when I commit my way to the Lord, whatever I do will prosper (Proverbs 16:3)!

When the world feels chaotic and out of control and the crippling effects of anxiousness attempt to detour me, God's Word continues to bring me confidence. I am promised, "My steps are being ordered by the Lord (Psalm 37:23)."

When I feel abandoned, broken, defeated or lost, I declared the promise, "When the righteous cry for help the Lord hears and delivers them out of all their troubles (Psalms 34:17)." He has always delivered me.

When the horrific memories of childhood molestation creep into my mind, and I am angered at the selfish and indecent person who took away a part of me that I never intended to give, I can be sure of this: "The wicked will **not** go unpunished, but those who are righteous will go free (Proverbs 11:12)."

When we were informed our newborn son had a hole in his heart and needed surgery, the spirit of fear tried to convince me Noah would never make it out alive. We gathered together a group of family and friends to agree and declare, Noah would live and not die. Within 72 hours the surgeon told us the hole was significantly smaller. The next week, surgeons determined no surgery was needed! Noah, who is now in his twenties gives his life to full time ministry. He travels all over the country sharing God's promises.

Even in the midst of the heightened threats and assaults to my faith, I can and I will declare the promises of God!

Are you broken? His words can heal you. Feeling lost? Let His words find you and bring you home. Abused? He wants to rescue and restore you! Rejected? He died for you!

He is a Promise Keeper. Every promise He said was yours, you should claim!

Pray this . . .
Father, I recognize although we live in the world, we do not wage war as the world does. You said, "the weapons I fight with are no match to the world's. On the contrary, they have <u>divine power to demolish strongholds</u>." I use the authority of Your Word to overcome any mindset not in complete alignment with Your truth. I declare a power of victory in every one of my circumstances that threaten to overwhelm me. While you renew my mind, I will praise You for delivering me. I will hide Your words in my heart so that I will not sin against you. I will use Your words to give direction to my future. Lord, The Word of God will forever be a beacon of hope and promise, for me and my seed. We will love Your word, obey Your word, honor Your word and teach Your word. In Jesus' name, the Word will be our constant foundation - Amen.

<u>#LetsGetReal</u>
Let's echo the words of Heaven and not earth! - Polly

#15
A CONTROLLED ENVIRONMENT

If you can't thank God for what you have, then thank Him for what you escaped. - Polly Herrin

David faced Goliath with no military experience and with nobody cheering him on! Strange to see a shepherd boy want to take on a giant, yet this God focused young man stood in a valley to face-off, even with the odds stacked against him. When all others cowered back in fear, David took on Goliath's challenge. He walked onto the battlefield and declared, *(and I am paraphrasing)* You come against me with a sword and spear, but I'm coming against you in the name of the Lord Almighty, the God of the armies of Israel. Today the Lord is delivering you into my hands. I will strike you down and cut off your head (I Samuel 17:45-47 NIV)!

Three Hebrew boys, Shadrach, Meshach and Abednego, were sentenced to the furnace to die by fire because they remained faithful to God. King Nebuchadnezzar came to witness their execution and in anger demanded the fire be turned up seven times hotter because the boys would not bow. Even when the flames grew higher and hotter, still no bowing happened that day (Daniel 3:8-25 NIV)! The Hebrew trio survived the fire and walked out with greater impact than they had going in. *Praise God.*

All brave souls face opposition that force you to make a deliberate stance against all that you feel and see, to side with the facts of Who you know!

Nobody promised this life would be without fights, flames and fire, and rarely will these tests and trials make sense to us. If they did, what purpose would faith have? God's desire is to build within you a warrior, who will bear His image and reflect His glory (Ephesians 1:11-14). This doesn't happen in comfortable, predictable, or safe places where we can keep things under control. It happens in places where it will require us to trust without understanding.

In I Peter 1:6-7 it says, "In this you can greatly rejoice, though now for a little while, if need be, you have been grieved by various trials, that the genuineness of your faith, being much more precious than gold that perishes, though it is tested by fire, may be found to praise, honor and glory at the revelation of Christ." Notice the phrase above, "If need be." This tells me, trials and tests are often initiated "If need be."

Let me try to explain it another way. Have you ever said something like this to your kids or maybe someone said this to you as a kid?

IF NEED BE, I will take that phone away from you.
IF NEED BE, we can take the car keys until you learn this lesson.
IF NEED BE, I'll spank your butt. *(Lol, my favorite.)*

God is a good Father, so IF NEED BE He <u>will</u> test your faith with the goal of refining you. He will do some things that may not feel good, to remove some things that aren't for your good.

God compares our testing to the process of precious metal being put in the fire in order to remove the impurities (Proverbs 25:4). For metal to have value, its' dross must be removed. According to the goldsmith these impurities cannot be seen in the metal before it hits the fire, at least not to the human eye; but when the heat is turned up, and the pressure is put on the gold, the impurities detach and rise to the surface. Twenty-four-carat gold is nearly one-hundred percent gold with very little impurities. Its value is <u>substantially greater than</u> that of a lower carat category, only <u>because it endured the fire longer.</u>

Do you feel like you've endured the fire a little longer? You absolutely need to know, your value is substantially increasing. **God is not mad at you, or finished with you; He is perfecting you!** When faced with something that seems as if it will burn you to the core, God is using it to push out things like fear, insecurity, unbelief, jealousy, anger, racism, pride and rebellion. Some things can't go with you to the next level, this process will remove them. Endure this test. It is an indicator that God is preparing you for your next upgrade.

Scripture Memorization
In all this you greatly rejoice, though now for a little while you may have had to suffer grief in all kinds of trials. These have come so that the proven genuineness of your faith—of greater worth than gold, which perishes even though refined by fire—may result in praise, glory and honor when Jesus Christ is revealed (I Peter1:6-7 NIV).

Reflection
While living in Florida, I had a group of friends I would walk and pray with on a bi-weekly basis. One walk I shared with my friend April. About half way through our total distance, we saw a huge ball of smoke billowing in the sky. Curious to know what was on fire, we took a detour to follow the smoke, landing us two blocks over. Upon arriving at the scene we saw emergency vehicles in rescue mode trying to extinguish a massive fire that had already engulfed several small buildings. Firefighters were pulling out hoses and issuing commands by loud speaker. Feeling an urgency that possibly lives may be in danger, April and I agreed we needed to start praying. Right there, we dropped to our knees and began to pray out-loud. *Me and my gang don't usually pray silently, and this day was no different!*

Not long into our prayer, I felt a tap on my shoulder. Looking up I saw a firefighter who chuckled before he spoke. He said, "Ladies, before you get too in prayer, I just wanted to make sure you saw the sign." He pointed to the fence at the side of the property. We hadn't noticed the sign, it was a good distance off on a fence that surrounded the property. He pointed again, and time we saw it. The sign read**, Training In Progress. This is a testing center!** Reaching down to help us up from our knees he continued, "Ladies, there is nothing to worry about. This burn is a controlled fire. We intentionally set that house on fire so our team could practice putting it out."

Ya'll, I have never been so embarrassed in my life! April and I darted out of there as quickly as we could. All the way home we laughed so hard it hurt. We vowed to never share this embarrassing moment with anyone. *Sorry April!*

God used this experience to teach me something extraordinary. He allowed me to see into a realm of wisdom I had not yet realized. **You see, things weren't as they appeared. Even when it looked like the flames were out of control, they were burning the house in a <u>controlled</u> <u>environment</u>!** God reminded me on that June summer day, we too are in a controlled environment. Every opposition, every battle, every trial, everything that feels as if it is wreaking havoc in your life, is completely under His Sovereign watch.

GIRL, YOU ARE FENCED IN! Surrounded by His authority, you have nothing to fear. He is diligently watching over your refining process. He knows exactly how long you need to endure. Rejoice, though for a little while, if need be you have to suffer, but ultimately know this fire is burning off all your restrictions and removing unhealthy attachments that have the potential to destroy your future. When you come through, God's image will be clearly visible on your life and increase will be inevitable.

Pray this . . .
Lord, Help me to stay in the fire. I know Your promise is to refine me, so if You allowed this trial, You have a reason. It has to be for my good. Give me the strength to go through it. Regardless of how hot the heat may feel, and no matter how unjust the flames may seem, I will not quit, because you promise there is good to come of this. It will strip away those things that have diminished my ability to go to the next level. I will have valuable insight, increased faith and Your glory will be evident in my life. I declare Isaiah 61:7, that through this experience I will exchange my shame with of joy, and the worth of my inheritance will double. All of my days are held in Your hands. Amen.

#LetsGetReal:
You may have lost a lot in the fire, but your destiny is not tied to what you lost, it's tied to what's left. - Polly

#16
WE FELT IT

__Holding on is not always a sign of being strong. Sometimes it takes more strength to let go. - Polly Herrin__

It's okay to <u>not</u> be okay!

David, a mighty warrior, chosen by God, favored and anointed, but he was still human. He was given the title, "A man after God's own heart," but who also had explosive outbursts of anger and prayed for God to destroy his enemies. In Psalm 109, David is heard asking God to, "number his enemies' days and to make them fatherless." Go read it for yourself. *Wow!* Are you just as surprised but also thankful that David would be so *real* to admit he wants his enemies to pay for all wrong? Reading some of his prayers make me look like an angel. Seriously, it encourages me that I too, can be *real* with God. He can handle it.

I'm learning it's okay to not be okay with the person who abused you, who didn't keep their promise, or made life a living hell. You're not wrong about those people, so stop questioning it.

God created each of us with an incredibly sensitive protection mode. He made you keen to danger, and with the ability to respond. Just as God uses people for His glory, satan will use them to accomplish his mission, and those willing to participate with the enemy, do not deserve influence in your life. Set a boundary. If no one told you yet, you're allowed to remove them from your front row! Make them get up. In the past, I was misguided by good people who suggested that boundaries were <u>un</u>-Christian. Years later with the help of professional Christian counseling, and through personal experience I now know boundaries are necessary and biblical (I Corinthians 15:33)! Don't ever be duped into thinking you need to open the door of your mind, heart, home, or family to sinister people. **<u>The devil is a liar!</u>**

Some things we nurture, but some have to be neutered.

Real evil is rampant in this world. Not everyone you meet strives for, kindness, reconciliation, and the truth, and allowing those people access to you is a casualty waiting to happen. You may suggest, aren't we commanded to forgive? <u>Absolutely you must forgive!</u> But there is a very thin line that separates boundaries and forgiveness. Being violated by someone who continues to show no remorse, is not healthy. Forgiveness shouldn't be an open door for people to take advantage of us. Forgiveness is releasing our offender to God so that we are able to walk away from retaliating. As a Survivor myself, I recognize many of you are in the same dilemma where I have been. You think if you forgive them it will nullify what they did, and they will do it again. I've been there between the crossroads of holding on and letting go. I hear ya, I've forgiven and I've tried to forget. Was it easy? No. Do I feel completely healed of the incident? Not yet! When you forgive it doesn't always mean you feel better. Sometimes forgiving costs more upfront than presumed, but I can promise you this, it is obedience unto God and He takes notice!

God has not turned a blind eye to the injustice you endured. He saw when the enemy tried to set you up. He heard it, when the truth was intentionally distorted to damage your character. When you were slighted a position, a reward, or an opportunity you deserved God acknowledge it. When you were wrongfully broken, abused, or mistreated He witnessed it. And when you turned the other cheek, <u>He felt it!</u>

Letting go and moving on with no expectation of an apology can require one of the highest forms of faith for a believer. <u>I'm sorry they never apologized.</u> I'm sorry they were selfish with their words. I'm sorry their evil acts took something away you can never get back. I'm sorry you have been suffering alone. You can't edit your reality, but you can decide to let God vindicate on your behalf (Psalm 37:6-8).

The clock is ticking on the enemy, and his time is almost up. He will pay!

Scripture Memorization
The acts of the flesh are obvious: sexual immorality, impurity and debauchery; idolatry and witchcraft; hatred, discord, jealousy, fits of rage, selfish ambition, dissensions, factions and envy; drunkenness, orgies, and the like. I warn you, as I did before, that those who live like this will <u>not</u> inherit the kingdom of God (Genesis 5:19-21 NIV) .

Reflection
Forgiving someone releases you from the need to retaliate, but not from the need to set a boundary. Abuse, of any kind, should never be justified. And if you are experiencing abuse, I pray you find the strength to walk away from those who will not take responsibility for their behavior, and then go and tell somebody. Some people have no desire to reconcile because these spirits are unwilling to repent and will not own responsibility. Sometimes the only way to heal is to set a boundary to limit your involvement to the people bent on hurting you. These people have far deeper issues than you can help. Find a trustworthy friend who will support you through it. Seek professional counseling or help from a church counselor or pastor. Whatever you do, don't walk this road alone.

Fight through the un-forgiveness, because you deserve to be free. Give it to God! He is more than able to restore what the enemy tried to destroy, and in His care your heart can heal. You will get stronger and the memories get weaker.

Pray this . . .
Honestly Lord, I've replayed past experiences in my mind of those people who should have treated me better, but didn't. I've rehearsed the "evil act" more times than I wanted. It's like a bad nightmare that won't quit. HELP ME LORD! I know without your help I will never move forward. Without you erasing the wound from my soul, I won't survive. I need your strength because I am weak. I need your wisdom, because my next move feels unknown.

Today, I draw a boundary line and I declare supernatural protection. I discharge angels to stand guard at the gate of my heart, thwarting back the enemies' attacks. Every trace of evil and spiritual wickedness sent to destroy me (or mine), will be destroyed. No remnant of evil will have access to me (or mine). Satan, you have NO authority here, the Holy Spirit resides in this space. No more will you be allowed to harass, taunt or maim me. It ends today.

God, I've been tempted to retaliate towards those who done me wrong, especially those who caused trauma _____(name it/child hood trauma, etc). The secret sin inflicted upon me and mine feels like it will never be punished. In my flesh I want to tell *her* off, I want to expose *him* publicly! *They've* taken so much from me I sometimes pray like David, *they* be destroyed, right in front of my eyes. Forgive me Lord and help me to forgive them. Walk with me through this.

Help me manager my emotions. I know it's not Your will that I wallow in brokenness so I declare I am rising up healed and restored. I will never again face off with this enemy - Amen.

Note: *I have never received an apology from the worst offender in my life, but I have received healing, and restoration. I can promise you this, healing and restoration from God, is far better than an apology.*

#LetsGetReal
Be okay with not sharing your side of the story, God heard every conversation and He witnessed every evil deed. He saw when you turned the other cheek. He will vindicate. - Polly

#17
KNOW YOUR WORTH

*God gave you an invitation to the table, now take your seat!
You belong here. - Polly Herrin*

Remember the story of Jacob, the grandson of Abraham and the son of Isaac? Jacob tricked his own father out of his brother's birthright. He lived up to his name, don't you think? His name was his handicap because Jacob means *trickster*! He was destined to be who they called him, until one day God changed his name from Jacob to Israel. And from that day forward the curse was reversed!

If you've read the Old Testament you've probably read at least a dozen times, the generational blessing directed to **Abraham, Isaac, and Jacob**. When God would use this phrase (Abraham, Isaac, and Jacob) we are told He was reminding His people of the covenant blessing He commanded on them and their descendants. The promise of seed, land and blessings, according to God, belonged to them forever!

If this generational blessing was to be echoed forever, then it provokes one to question: God changed Jacob's name to Israel, then shouldn't the areas of the bible that address **"Abraham, Isaac, and Jacob"** instead read, **"Abraham, Isaac, and Israel?"** *Hang with me, I really want you to get this.* If God changed Jacob's name to Israel, shouldn't we be saying and reading, **"Abraham, Isaac, and Israel?"** And, if you're the God who wants to make Yourself known wouldn't you use the new name Israel in place of Jacob? Israel is the name change symbolizing a new identity. It's the man without the labels and mistakes. Israel is the *better* version of Jacob. So why keep Jacob's name in the line of blessing?

I believe God intentionally left Jacob's name in the blessing because He wanted you and I to know, He's the God of Jacob too! By leaving in the name Jacob, God wanted us to remember that our struggles can't define us, and our past will not limit us.

The world may suggest you need to act a certain way to get the invite, but God says, just come as you are! The world requires you to earn your seat at the table, by the works of your hands. Jesus declared, He already did the work on an old rugged cross. You don't have to earn anything, it's already been paid in full.

Stop letting the world convince you otherwise. Take your seat at this family table, where generational blessings are forever yours. You belong here. No matter what failures line the resume of your past, God still intends to bless your future. Now live like it (*period*)!

Scripture Memorization
But you are a **chosen people**, a royal priesthood, a holy nation, God's special possession, that you may declare the praises of Him who called you out of darkness into His wonderful light (I Peter 2:9 NIV).

Reflection
There is real pain in living underestimated. When we allow the world to underestimate us it not only affects our present, but it halts the potential of our future. Avoid looking to other voices to validate you. God believes in you. If God has identified you as redeemed, forgiven, victorious, overcomer, blessed, favored, chosen, and set apart - then why in the heck would you listen to somebody like *Uncle Bob*?! *Uncle Bob* may have identified some experiences you've been through, and some mistake you made, but it's not who you are. Your experiences do not define you. Remove those constrictive labels and free yourself from wrong words and unsolicited opinions.

The gospel isn't a do, do, do, and then do some more - nope, it's done! Salvation isn't a goal for Christians, it's a gift. You don't have to prove who you are; He already qualified you, and by the shedding of His blood, He proved who you could become!

Pray this . . .
God, I've lost my way. I've allowed the mistakes of my past to exempt me from Your grace. I've accepted the opinions of others and allowed them to limit me. In search of gaining their approval I have slowly abandoned my pursuit in pleasing You. Forgive me. Crucify my desire to find acceptance in this fickle world. Cleanse my heart of all hard moments, hard people, and harsh words that keep me in bondage. My mistakes don't define me, because You died to free me. Instead of broken, You call me healed. Instead of weak, You call me strong. Instead of unloving, You call me loved. Instead of lost, You call me found.

Forgetting those things behind me, I press on to fulfill the purpose You have for my life. I am victorious. I am chosen. I am invited. I am worthy. I am significant and I belong. I am the righteousness of Christ, made in Your image. Blessed. Prosperous. Healthy. Wise. Favored. Everything You said I could be, I will become. Nothing can separate me from Your love - Amen.

#LetsGetItRight
Know your worth, then add tax! - Polly

#18
ENVY NEVER CLAPS

One of life's greatest tests will be how you handle those who mishandled you. - Author Unknown

*In this devotional I share about a time when I participated in the character assassination of someone who meant a lot to me. I'm not proud of this behavior, but I still choose to share my admission of wrongdoing, in hopes that the Holy Spirit will use the error of my ways to prevent others from engaging in behavior that has eternal consequences. *Names have been changed to keep privacy.*

Years ago, in my circle of ministry friends, there was a younger pastor's wife I became friends with and eventually mentored. I'll call her *Sadie* for privacy purposes. She would call often for insight and suggestions on parenting and ministry. I really loved that *Sadie* trusted me with her questions. Although at that time we lived a few hours from one another, thanks to the invention of *FaceBook*, our friendship bloomed. I felt privileged when *Sadie* asked me to take on the role as one of her mentors. I happily invested a lot into the friendship, but the rewards of her admiration and pure appreciation for my help, was also a blessing to me. I felt a deep soul connection with *Sadie*. I was here for it.

Fast forward a few years later, *Sadie* and her husband began to see expansion in many areas of their lives. Their ministry exploded, her personal career grew, and her influence on social media was unstoppable. And about that same time, it was difficult getting calls through to *Sadie*. My attempts either went to voicemail or they were intercepted by her new "assistant." Getting the feeling *Sadie* no longer needed some of the same support she received from me prior to her new season of popularity. I was a little bitter. *Okay, maybe a lot bitter.*

Not long after while attending a luncheon with some of *Sadie's* mutual friends, her name came up in conversation. One by one they echoed the same feelings of hurt. It was obvious we all felt the sting of rejection now that *Sadie* had found her new tribe, and it seemed she'd left us behind. The conversation became malevolent and what once started as a way to vent frustration, quickly digressed to murder . . . **murder by mouth!** It was evident our choice of words reflected tainted hearts of envy and jealousy towards *Sadie*.

I want to stop right here and talk *real*: slandering a person's character, even if what is stated is true, always displeases God and will bring severe consequences to those who do. The Bible makes it clear in James 3:16, "Where there is <u>envy</u> and <u>jealousy</u> you will find <u>every</u> kind of evil." Pause and let's take note of the word "every." God used the word "every" to explain that evil of all kinds will attach itself to you when you hold envy and jealousy towards someone! *(Read it again!)* I don't know about you, but it's hard enough to wrestle one wrong spirit, so why would I intentionally invite <u>every</u> evil spirit into my life? Yet that's exactly what we do when we harbor envy and jealousy. Unchecked it grows and contaminates more than you have the power to control.

We can not let our guard down! Even within "Christian circles" there are many opportunities to participate in erosive environments. I've served under prideful leaders, so envious of another's gifts they intentionally withheld an opportunity and recognition because of their own insecurities. Their unwillingness to publicly applaud and give honor to others created an undermining and weakened team that lead to tangible evidence of division. This once talented, thriving, team with unlimited potential, was now vulnerable to the same spirits and eventually began to devour one another. *(Heartbreaking!)*

Closed fists, closed mouths, closed wallets and closed hearts never align with God's plan. Jesus said, "It is more blessed to give than to receive." Limiting what you give to others looks nothing like Jesus.

Jesus gave it <u>ALL</u> so we could have a step up. Not just a step up, but a step out; out of the grips of hell, and eternal damnation! Not because we even deserved it, but because He loved us while we were still sinning. Freely you have received, now freely give (Matthew 10:8)!

When she exceeds in any area of life, <u>clap</u> for her!

When she takes the promotion or opportunity you wanted, go ahead and <u>clap</u> for her!

When she changes social and economic circles, <u>clap</u> for her!

When she defies the odds and creates something that positions her to be known, <u>clap</u>, <u>clap</u>, and <u>clap</u> some more.

Go ahead and stand up and <u>clap</u> for her! (Let's just do it!)

Don't rush past this devo! God help me explain how you want it to be heard.

God said many of you will still excuse yourself from this simple act of honor. You will remain selective in who you applaud, invite, encourage and promote. This resistance shows a spirit of pride, that He cannot honor when you remain stingy with your kindness! It's easy to show kindness to those who reciprocate, but the real test of a pure heart, gives first with no expectation of ever receiving anything back.

When we stay "green with envy" we will choose to withhold applause, praise, opportunity and encouragement from others. These types of seemingly hidden behaviors are visible to God, and will block every blessing!

King Saul was once chosen by God and living with His visible favor of blessing, until he became envious of the next King in line. Saul never dealt with his jealousy towards David and it turned into hatred. This cruel emotion made him unable to think straight and he became careless and vindictive! Eventually Saul murdered himself and everything attached to him paid the consequence for his unrestrained sin.

Be on guard against the enemy's schemes to enslave you to envy and jealousy. I can promise you the consequences will not be worth the investments.

Scripture Memorization
A heart at peace gives life to the body, but envy rots the bones (Proverbs 14:30).

Reflection
Note: I apologized to my friend Sadie. She was hurt but received my apology and quickly forgave me. I'm so thankful.

I personally believe un-forgiveness is a learned behavior. Toddlers don't hold grudges. One minute they can be arguing over a toy, and the next sharing peanut butter and jelly sandwiches. They live free of offense. But in environments where conflict and offenses are never dealt with, where un-forgiveness is allowed to operate, the fruit of division, jealousy, competition and bitterness will be hard to destroy.

We teach what we know, but we reproduce who we are.

Jesus gave us "The Lord's Prayer" in which to model how to ask for forgiveness and receive it. In Matthew 6:12 (NLT) He teaches us to pray, **"forgive us our sins, <u>as we have forgiven those</u> who sin against us!"** Have you ever stopped to consider this prayer you pray? I have. It's sobering.

Do you really want God to forgive you in the same way you forgive others? Let me ask it this way: do you really want God to forgive you like you've forgiven? Do you want Him to forgive you, like you forgave the parent who abandoned you? Or the spouse that cheated on you? Or the friend that slandered you? Because Jesus said, in whatever way and depth you forgive those people, He forgives you. *Yikes!*

Jesus then goes on to give us more warning in verses 14 and 15, **"If you forgive those who sin against you, your heavenly Father will forgive you, but if you refuse to forgive others, your Father will <u>not</u> forgive your sins." (NLT)**

Don't be angry with me friend, those are words written in red. I'm just the messenger, it's His message! According to Jesus, forgiving others is not an option. If we desire forgiveness and a "right" standing with God, we must forgive as God forgives, quickly and completely. It's not our job to stand in as "Judge" and determine if they are worthy of forgiveness. And it's definitely not okay to make them pay by punishing them in some way for their wrongdoing. **You are not really forgiving if there are conditions to your forgiveness!**

Jesus tells a story in Matthew 18 about a man who had a huge debt. The man couldn't pay it back, so the king decided to throw him in prison and sell his family into slavery. The Matthew 18 guy begs for mercy, and amazingly the king pardons him completely. Even the debt he owed was erased. Later, this same Matthew 18 guy encounters someone who owes him a lot less money but he refuses to forgive the debt. His anger is unleashed. He seeks punishment and puts the man in prison.

Are you like the Matthew 18 guy? When your child makes the mistake, you beg for mercy; but when it's my child you want justice. If I offend you, you justify the silent treatment; but when you offend me, I'm just being too sensitive. When you sin, you choose to hide it; but when it's somebody else's sin, you decide it needs to be exposed. See here's the thing . . .

When my sin bothers you more than your sin, you have forgotten all about grace!

We need to remember what we've been forgiven of before we limit the forgiveness we give. God didn't just overlook your sins, He took your sins and hung them on the cross and declared, "Father forgive them for they know not what they do!" Your sin was forgiven, **not because you deserved it,** but because He loved you in spite of it. Don't go withholding that same gift from others.

To be forgiven, one must completely forgive.

Pray this . . .
This one is difficult, but I know we can do this.

Dear God, I haven't always treated others with kindness, nor have I lived my life without envy. At times my heart has been bitter, unkind and vindictive. I've been quick to hold on to offense. I've even withheld opportunities and compliments when I should have been the first to stand and applaud. I've sat in circles where envy was served as the main meal, and sadly I took a bite. Forgive me, Lord! What I have selfishly ruined, I ask You to heal and restore.

To those who were envious of me and their actions proved it, I forgive you! To those who with unkind words murdered my character and assassinated my reputation, I forgive. To those who caused division and sought to hurt me, I forgive. To those who refused to forgive me, and continue in some way to punish me, I forgive. I do not want to be bound to this madness any longer. I am free, because I have freely forgiven.

Heal these soul hurts. The hidden betrayal, unjust accusations, slander, disrespect, dishonor, abuse (physical, sexual, emotional) _____(fill in your hurt), I give to You God. I don't know how to manage it anymore. I am weary and worn but I will be obedient to forgive knowing You will keep Your promise to avenge (Deuteronomy 32:35).

At times turning the other cheek is a hard discipline to follow and seems unfair. When I linger too long in my negative thoughts and start to rationalize why I shouldn't forgive, please help me to remember you went to the cross for me when I didn't deserve it. Your love is amazing. You gave love before I was ever willing to receive it. Thank You, Lord!

#LetsGetReal
Someone else's victory is not your defeat! - Polly

#19
YOU ARE MORE THAN

When you have the attention of God, you will also have the attention of the enemy. - Author Unknown

Being favored by God can bring about unwanted attacks you didn't ask for. Joseph was favored by his earthly Father and his Heavenly Father. His earthly father gave him an expensive coat of many colors, and his Heavenly Father gave Joseph dreams that promised him rule and reign. Both attracted unwanted attention from his jealous brothers. Anger rose up within them, and their wicked plot, landed Joseph in a pit that left him for dead (Genesis 37).

This world is fickle in its allegiance to loyalty and love. One minute you can be somebody's favorite, and the next they can cancel you, stuff you in a hole and put a lid on it. Don't take it too personal. They may succeed today in isolating you, and excluding opportunities from you, with the goal to get rid of you, but God's plan always prevails.

You can't be canceled, Darling!

God's plan for your life isn't contingent on the world's approval. I can tell you that all day, but it doesn't matter as much until you start believing it for yourself! Something sacred happens when you comprehend that being set aside is really being set apart for God's service. When you are set apart for the King, understand you may be misunderstood, but obedience to the call is non-negotiable.

Resist the temptation to limit your potential just because the world can't see it. God has big plans in your future. God promises every area of your life can exceed your expectations, immeasurably more than you could even imagine (Ephesians 3:20), so expect it!

Let me remind someone:

> You are more than any setback trying to discourage you!
> You are more than the person who refused to accept you!
> You are more than the diagnosis sent to distract you!
> You are more than the past that tries to remind you!
> You are more than the fear that threatens you!
> You are more than the tongue that slanders you!
> You are more than the limits which have restricted you!
> You are more than the labels that have been assigned to you!
> You are more than the opportunity that was stripped from you!
> You are more than the mirror reflects back to you!

Cease wasting another God given day searching for accolades in frivolous places. You were created to conquer (Romans 8:37). You are absolutely more than _____ *(Fill in the blank)* because God said you were. And that fact will never change whether the world believes it or not!

Scripture Memorization
If the world hates you, keep in mind that it hated Me first. If you belonged to the world, it would love you as its own. As it is, you do not belong to the world, but I have chosen you out of the world. That is why the world hates you. Remember what I told you: A servant is not greater than his master. If they persecuted me, they will persecute you also. (John 15:18-20 NIV).

Reflection
We are a society who craves approval. We shop for validation on social media platforms, filling our carts with "likes and loves!" Still, some can never get enough and become part of the vicious cycle of **those who spend their efforts searching for worth from a world who isn't able to see it.**

A sweet rush of approval from the world, is fleeting. To truly live free from limitations, you have to break away from other's opinions. Get up from tables where you still beg to belong and where respect is no longer being served. You deserve more!

Believe in yourself!

You are an amazing masterpiece, created without a duplicate. You are so unique that even your fingerprint is one of a kind. With great intention God designed you for a purpose that only you can fulfill. He ultimately sealed your worth by sending His only Son to die for you, making the price paid incalculable by human hands. You are chosen! You are significant!

Others may try to limit you, but Girl, don't you dare limit yourself!

My prayer for you: Father, I pray for those reading this who have been battling so long and hard they are weary to the point of exhaustion. Their hope has been diminished because of the repetitive attacks sent one after the other, with no time to be restored and strengthened. The enemy continuously fights against their will to believe they are worth love. Intervene and put an end to his lies. May Your unconditional love override the limitations they feel and remind them

Your plan can only be cancelled if they stop participating in it. Oh God, I see many who need to be delivered from the wrong circles and set in the right ones. Give discernment to allow them to see the warning signs. Pull them up from pits where they were left to die and position them for elevation. Then, as only You can do, open doors for them like you did for Joseph. Make a way with no restrictions allowed. Your favor follows them, elevation is finding them, and peace surrounds them. In the name of Jesus we pray - Amen.

Personal Declaration
I am worthy.
I am valuable.
I am significant.
I am loved.
I am victorious.

I am positioned for greatness and You will lead me to prosperous opportunities.
I am more than! Oh, yes I am!
I am an overcomer, sealed with purpose and promise.

#LetsGetReal:
The words you say to yourself are more important than the words others say about you. - Polly

#20
MADE TO WAIT

The only time I regretted waiting on God, was when I didn't.
- Author Unknown

Recently in my alone time with God, I've thought about all the answers He's given to my questions and the provisions He's made. Impossible situations became victories because God made a way! I am again convinced today, He's got my other requests covered. But if I'm completely honest, I feel some of the prayers took a long time to answer. I struggled staying patient in the waiting. Especially when the need or problem seemed bigger than life and stifled any hope I had left. I'm not proud about the times I lived in unbelief. Thank God He didn't hold it against me. He still showed up every single time!

Jesus is heard telling a parable in Luke 18 of a poor, powerless women who persists in nagging a corrupt, powerful judge to do justice for her. She desperate and she needed a miracle. Perseverance is a key component to our faith. Shameless in her pleading, this woman wasn't turned back by the rejection of the wait. You see the enemy is terrified of that kind of faith. That's why he tries to convince you prayer is wasted time. He absolutely knows it only takes one move from God and He will reorder the chaos in your life, heal infirmities, take down giants, destroy strongholds, multiply what's left and save what's lost! I am living proof.

During a waiting season it's easy to get discouraged and begin to question God. Especially when it seems He has chosen to stay silent and inactive. Galatians 6:9 challenges us "to not grow weary in doing good." It then goes on to say, "for in due season we will reap, if we do not give up." We all could benefit from learning the discipline of waiting. It's hard to do. That's exactly why I believe the second part of the promise in Galatians 6:9 is so important. Our waiting has a "due season". What does that mean? The word *due* is defined, "expected or planned for a certain time." Simply put, your due season can't be delayed! It has a set time to meet its expected purpose. Like a mother carrying new life in the womb, that baby will come when it's ready and there will be no stopping it. **God has a due season for you and nothing can stop it.** We need to make that *phrase* a part of our normal language during those long periods when it seems nothing is happening, and we've done our best to be obedient to God. We have to press in and persevere. Especially when you are weary and tired.

Daniel did this well. His people were oppressed for almost seventy years. This famous Old Testament prophet fasted on their behalf. For twenty-one days he labored in prayer for his people, but received no response. Then on day twenty-two the breakthrough arrived. An angel of God appeared. He revealed to Daniel the reason for the long delay. The angel said, "The prince of the Persian kingdom resisted me twenty-one days (Daniel 10:13 NLT)."

For twenty-one days it seemed nothing was happening but from Heaven's perspective a war was taking place! Make no mistake about it, the moment Daniel uttered his first word for help, God was fighting on his behalf. When you pray all of Heaven is waging war on your behalf. God's angels are engaged and attentive to His requests. Jesus is seated at the right hand of the Father making intercession for you. You may not see anything happening, but I can promise you - something is happening!

God is not sometimes Sovereign, nor is He randomly victorious. He doesn't occupy the throne one day and take a break the next. He is the King of kings and Lord of all, every single day!

Are you tempted with a distracted mind and a heavy burden wondering if God is capable, and still able to fulfill the promise? I want you to hear a resounding, "Yes, He is!" God is more than able. So take a deep breath, exhale your praise to Him. He is faithful! It will be worth the wait.

Scripture Memorization
Now to Him who is able to do immeasurably more than all we ask or imagine, according to His power that is at work within us, to Him be

glory in the church and in Christ Jesus throughout all generations, for ever and ever! Amen (Ephesians 3:20-21 NIV).

Reflection

In Matthew 7:11 Jesus said, "If you then, being evil, know how to give good gifts to your children, how much more will your Father in Heaven give good gifts to those who ask Him."

I love giving gifts to my children, don't we all? But sometimes I've wanted to give them something but they aren't ready for it. Let me give you an example: My daughter Karson received a valuable one carat blue sapphire from her Nana Barb on her twelfth birthday. When she opened the gift, she gasped out loud and held her heart. "It's gorgeous, Nana Barb. Thank you" she said. Taking it out of the box with care she then put the ring on, but it didn't fit. It dangled around those tiny, immature fingers. Realizing she was not ready for this gift, I told Karson we were going to put her precious ring in a "safe place" until she was older. And that's exactly what we did. Locked away and protected, her ring was secured with other the items we deemed valuable.

In the months to come, Karson would repeatedly ask to wear her ring. I think her pestering was more obsessive than the woman mentioned in Luke 18. *(Seriously, she doesn't give up easily.)* I had remind Karson she wasn't mature enough for the gift, not just yet. "Mom that's my ring. Nana Barb gave it to me, and I should be able to wear it when I want," she argued her point. I certainly understood her frustration but I wasn't withholding this gift because I was trying to punish my daughter. I knew it was her ring, but in reality, she was too young to understand the value of this gift! Besides, her finger still needed to grow for the ring to fit appropriately or she would risk loosing it.

Karson is a senior in college. She seasonally moves in and out of our home, but when she finally moves out for good *(I don't want that to happen any time soon),* that beautiful ring will go with her. Her Nana's gift will solely be in her possession to wear as she wishes.

Are you frustrated and impatient with God? Have you lost hope because He said the promise was yours, but you have yet to receive it? Be encouraged, His delays are not always denials. The gift (the promise) is on the way. It's not gone, it's being protected. It's always been yours, He's just preparing you for it.

You don't have to prove God's promises, you just have to believe them. God will do what He said He would do!

Pray this . . .
Lord, honestly, I am over the wait! I don't know how I will endure another day of waiting! It's hard to believe that the promise is still on the way, when nothing in my life reflects that it is. Help me to believe in spite of what I see. Please give me supernatural discernment to see with eyes of understanding and a steadfast confidence to trust You are working on my behalf. Prepare my heart to receive what You are doing. In the midst of my troubles, send Your peace to settle my soul. And please, increase my faith to believe my harvest will not delay a single day longer than it's determined time.

You are a good Father! You have gifts and promises for me that have not yet been fulfilled, but are intended to exceed my expectations. According to Jeremiah 29:11, Your plans for me are to prosper me. I will live to see that prosperous plan unfold. Oh Sovereign God, You are faithful to a thousand generations! You are the overseer of every area of my life and the appointed promise shall not delay. The promise is irrevocable. I call it mine - Amen.

#LetsGetReal
I'd rather repeat my prayer to God a thousand times than to give the enemy the satisfaction of my silence. - Polly

#21
THE TABLES ALWAYS TURN

Some people will try to expose what's wrong with you because they can't stand what's right about you. Keep doing you. - Bishop Jakes

Joseph's brothers were insanely jealous of their father's love for the last born kid, and to make matters worse, Joseph wasn't humble about it. Can you visualize him running out to the fields? Tanned skin, red cheeks, and a big mouth flaunting his special coat. He enters the scene arrogantly shouting, "Hey brothers, I had a dream and one day soon, you will be bowing down to me. Oh and by the way, look what Daddy just gave me! My new fine coat with a plethora of many colors. . .do ya'll have one?" Joseph's bold vision turned his family against him, and his arrogance fueled their emotions to anger.

Take notice, when the mark of God is on your life, the enemy will put a target in the same place. He will almost always schedule an "assassin" to murder the dream before it ever comes to life. Be selective in who you share your dreams with, because not everyone is capable of celebrating them.

Family turned to foes can sometimes be the hardest heartache to get over. Joseph's brothers couldn't stand the way their father loved him. Sure, he wasn't the easiest guy to live with, but did that justify him being thrown in a pit, sold to merchants for pocket change, and left for dead. It sure looked as if their evil plans were succeeding.

Over the next decade Joseph experienced more heartbreak and false accusations that landed him in jail. Unfair treatment seemed to be the trademark of his life. This series of unfortunate events caused by others looked like it was spiraling out of control. But God's hand was always on Joseph. Positioning him in places of favor, he eventually was promoted to second in command, serving directly under Pharaoh.

A famine was on the rise, and Joseph's brothers were a part of a large caravan of hungry people headed to Egypt. Desperate for food, their need brought them back to the only person that could help them, Joseph! Here, they stood before the brother they once betrayed, to ask for help.

The tables turned - they always do!

We've all experienced betrayal. We know unfair and we know injustice. It hurts. When we've been done wrong the most natural response is to want to retaliate, and satan will try everything to get us involved. Don't give in to his temptation! God cares about justice more than we do. Besides, He said there were two things He would never share: His vengeance (Romans 12:19) and His glory (Isaiah 42:8). Vindication is God's act alone, He doesn't want our help. More importantly, when we avenge ourselves God will let us, but we will be without His protection.

The visible favor and anointing on your life will attract attacks, because your obedience to the mission makes you hated. Your hell-like experience may seem unending, and you may not have an ounce of hope left to believe God can do something about your situation, but you are so wrong. **Don't let the middle of your story confuse you.** God is so much bigger than all of your preconceived notions of how to "manage" Him. Let Him work. Resist the urge to vindicate yourself and allow God to beautifully orchestrate your victory.

You carry greatness within you, something the world needs. Live your life in obedience to God, and He will turn it around. You will get to the palace. You will fulfill your destiny.

Scripture Memorization
. . .This is what the Lord says to you: 'Do not be afraid or discouraged because of this vast army. For the battle is not yours, but God's (2 Chronicles 20:15b NIV).

Reflection

People will sometimes be unforgiving and hold you to a higher standard. People may use you for their own gain. Some may plot evil against you in hopes you will fail. People will leave you out to limit opportunities. People will lie *to* you and *about* you. These behaviors only prove one thing: **People are in need of a Savior!**

Stay free from resentment and bitterness. Those poisonous emotions locked up inside of you never bring justice; they will only make you sick. Steady your heart on this truth—He saw you turn the other cheek, and every moment your heart was broken, He witnessed it. Your pain hasn't escaped His view and soon, He will turn the tables if you remain free of offense. The quickest way to position yourself in the place where God can elevate you, is to bless your enemies (Matthew 5:4). Start now. Pray for your enemies and learn to bless those who curse you. *Nope, that's not a misprint!*

God said you need to bless those that curse you and do harm to you, and while you're doing it, bless them well. Will it be easy? Heck, no! Must we do it? Absolutely yes. The bible warns that offenses will come, but the choice to hold on to the offense, or let it go, is up to you. One choice yields a reward of blessing, the other holds severe consequences. I pray you have the willpower to let it go! When you handle your hurt the way God requires, His unlimited favor will follow you. His blessings will chase you down. You will be positioned and elevated to the palace where greater things will fall into your destiny.

When you learn to turn the other cheek, God will turn the table in your favor.

I'm embarrassed to admit I've lived with un-forgiveness toward someone for years. Honestly, I didn't want this person back in my life and for good reasons! This person was harmful to my emotional well being, and whenever in their presence, I was vulnerable to these feelings. But my refusal to forgive was still wrong. The requirement to forgive an offender isn't an option, and it took me years to realize that staying offended was blocking my blessings. One day, at the advice of a friend, I wrote a letter to this person. You may be wondering why a letter? At this season in my life, I was afraid I would let my emotions get the best of me. Being a survivor of trauma by abuse, I tend to react like a survivor. I didn't want to be vulnerable to these feelings that could have the potential to jeopardize the intention to forgive and be forgiven. A letter was the better option. Before sending the letter I prayed over it, and then after three days, into the mailbox it went. I waited patiently for a response. Days passed, which then turned into weeks. Still no response. At first I was heartbroken, then angered, and before anger could turn into bitterness, I reached out to my mentor, the one who helped me draft the letter. I definitely needed to handle this correctly, so I sought her opinion. She said, "Polly, I'm sorry but I have a feeling this person is _not_ going to give you the closure you are wanting. It is the very reason you are at this pivotal moment. They've never wanted you to be free from this unhealthy cycle. Besides they have no accountability! Their lack of remorse is spiteful in many ways. You obeyed the Lord with the intent to reconcile. He saw that. But you may have to be okay with never getting a response back." Ughhhhh - do you hear my heartbreak? My feelings and self-worth were once again mishandled. My friend was correct. It seemed this cycle would never end. How could a professing Christian not want to reconcile! It took me awhile to get to the place of true forgiveness, with this one.

Forgiveness can seem unfair, especially when the person shows no remorse at all! But their indifference, and lack of empathy have no reflection on you. That is their problem and they will have to answer to God. You must still forgive. It won't be easy, because hurt hearts never want to cooperate with holy instruction.

Bitter never gets better folks. Left to fester, it will detour you from the blessings of God. Let it go - just let it go! Give your hurtful memories and broken heart to God. Let Him handle them. He knows what happened and will address it all in equal measures of mercy and justice. Allow God to transform bitter into better so you can be blessed. Forgiveness will be the key.

God has elevation in your near future, and it could solely be dependent on your willingness to move past the offense and forgive.

I'm pretty sure if Joseph could pull up a chair at a table with us and share a cup of coffee, he would have much to say about the biblical discipline of forgiveness. I believe he would start by encouraging us to forgive quickly. Then I think he'd say: **Nobody can turn a table like God!** Wink! Wink!

My prayer for you: I pray every scheme of the enemy against you be arrested! Every attempt of manipulation to block you from God's purpose dismantled and defeated this very moment. What others have said about you, done to you, or may even be planning now against you, will have no authority over who God has called you. Let every negative, backbiting, accursed word said against you be silenced and rendered powerless. Your God given assignment may have attracted attacks, but now may an enduring spirit rise within you to finish your assignment. Despite what you see or hear, I pray it has no influence on what You believe. God will bless you as you go in, and He will bless you coming out. Every place your feet step will have dominion.

Be free from anxiety, fear, tormenting and delusional thoughts. Be at peace, body, soul, mind and spirit as the Spirit of God covers you with wisdom and favor. The King of Glory, The Almighty One, who has all power is fighting for you, and when He fights, He always wins. You are walking in victory! Every enemy you see today, will be no more - Amen.

#LetsGetItRight:
Every enemy has an expiration date! - Polly

#22
PRESS THE MUTE BUTTON

The ones who say "you can't" and "you won't" are probably really the ones scared that you will. - Beth Moore

After the fall, Adam desperately tried to explain to God he was ashamed because he was naked. I love the way God responded. He asked Adam, "Who told you that you were naked?" Obviously by his actions, Adam was influenced by a voice other than the voice of God. Up until this point, God never mentioned to Adam that he was "naked", although he had been naked the day before, and every one before that. So tell me, what voice convinced Adam he was naked?

God's intention was always that the earth would reflect heaven. That's why God said to pray, "Thy will be done on earth as it is in heaven." But sin entered the world by way of a slithering, malicious snake, who came to turn over paradise. From day one he wanted you to question God, and his tactics haven't changed. Satan knows if he can get you to live in unbelief, he can ultimately change your identity and steal everything God purposed for you.

Since day one, Satan has been taking every opportunity to distort God's words, one lie at a time. Satan's not after your car; he can't drive. He's not after your things; he can't use them. Satan doesn't want your money, because he has no way to spend it. Satan is after your mind to occupy it. He wants full control of your thoughts. He knows if he can distort the truth of God's word, he can get you to forfeit your future.

All dreams start in the mind. All decisions are made in the mind. The mind is exactly the area of greatest threat to your destiny. It is definitely a battlefield like no other. Imagine the grieving heart of your Heavenly Father as He watches you wrestle with the truth. Friend, you have given way too much attention to the voice of the enemy. None of his threats hold authority, so why are you still entertaining him? It's time you silence satan! You can start by reminding him of the empty tomb where Jesus buried every lie in the grave. In this victory, God gave you all authority to denounce the lie and trade it for His truth.

You have the power to change misaligned conversations and declarations according to Proverbs 18:21. Be proactive! Choose wisely who and what you listen to, because what you allow to have priority in your heart will come out in your speech, and your speech will prophesy your future. When thoughts go unexamined they can do detrimental damage. Negative thoughts left to roam will only lead to negative behavior. Let's stop believing everything we hear. If what you are hearing contradicts what God's word says, it's time to press the mute button. I pray this is the day you become brave enough to break free from unsolicited opinions. Don't waste another day incarcerated by the words God never spoke over you.

The enemy isn't the least bit threatened by your words, but He is bound by God's!

Prioritize them over your own words and that my friend, is how you win.

Scripture Memorization
So then faith comes by hearing, and hearing by the word of God (Romans 10:17 NKJV).

Reflection
Who told you it was too late to start over?
Who made you feel incapable, inadequate and unaccepted?
Who said you couldn't do it?
Who denied you forgiveness and a second chance?
Who told you it's too late?

It certainly was not God!

He said, "You are the head and not the tail." He declared, "You are an overcomer!" He gave you "all authority in heaven and on earth", and He promised "in your weakness you would be made strong." He said,

"Time and seasons were always in His hand." He promised, "to never leave you or forsake you" and He made provision for your future.

Guard and examine every singe word you receive and every one you speak. If it doesn't align with God's word, it's gotta go!

Pray this . . .
Lord, free me from the bully within. Free my from wrong perceptions. Free me from what's been said against me. Words of hate spewed from jealous hearts. Words of deceit spewed from a deceitful heart. Words of shame, spewed from a shame filled heart. These false accusations have made my heart their home far too long! I bind up these ominous and debilitating words sent to hold me hostage, and I make them submit to Your authority. They are no longer given permission to roam freely within the corridors of my soul. Anything that costs me my peace, must be muted!

Please heal the inner most part of my heart that has been wrecked up by reckless people! Restore to me the fulness of Your joy. Restore to me hope, peace and confidence. Greater are You (God) within me, than any voice spoken against me - Amen.

#LetsGetReal
Stop believing things God never said about you. - Polly

#23
SHE SLAYS GIANTS

The enemy will always come back to test the validity of your break through. - Polly Herrin

Remember the story of David and Goliath? David's father asked him to take some happy meals to his brothers who were serving in the military. He obeyed, and on this occasion, **obedience placed David right in the middle of a brutal war**! *(All those who doubt God may sometimes call His people to war, please read it again.)*

Until David arrived on the scene, not one of these so-called mighty soldiers had the confidence to face off with this uncircumcised Philistine. David remembered his tribe was chosen. He remembered God made a promise that every enemy standing against this nation He loved, would be cursed. Shocked and offended by this loud mouthed bully, and his degradation of Jehovah, David stepped up to confront the giant. He was by far the least qualified for this assignment. Small in stature and inexperienced in warfare, yet none of his limitations stopped him. Picking up five smooth stones, he set out to do work!

Before hurling the first stone into the air David boldly made this declaration, "You come against me with sword and spear and javelin, but I come against you in the name of the Lord Almighty, the God of the armies of Israel, whom you have defied. This day the Lord will deliver you into my hands, and I'll strike you down and cut off your head. This very day I will give the carcasses of the Philistine army to the birds and the wild animals, and the whole world will know that there is a God in Israel (I Samuel 17:45)."

I doubt David ever thought he was qualified to take on this giant, but he didn't have to be. He just showed up in obedience and remembered God was with Him. David acknowledged the magnitude of our great God and the giant went down! *Praise God.* With just one stone, and a shepherd boy's radical faith, an entire nation was preserved.

Many Christian circles are choosing to ignore the enemy and act as if he doesn't exist. Spiritual warfare is a reality in the life of every believer and there is no shortage of passages in the New Testament about the Christian life being focused on warriors in battles. Satan is most effective when he is not acknowledged and he knows it. You will never defeat an enemy that you refuse to admit exists.

You too, have been commissioned to the fight. You are called to slay generational giants that have bound your tribe to the uncircumcised. You may feel this assignment is weighty and overwhelming, it is - but you can't sit on the sidelines in fear and wish the enemy away. He's not going anywhere! He's staying on your territory until you make him leave.

Scripture Memorization
Praise the Lord, who is my Rock, <u>who trains my hands for war, my fingers for battle.</u> He is my loving God and my fortress, my stronghold and my deliverer, my shield, in whom I take refuge, who subdues peoples under me (Psalm 144:1-2 NIV).

Reflection
Most giant slayers I've met have been threatened! Repeatedly threatened by all types of bullies; generational, religious, and territorial. Left to grow and advance these spirits will become more aggressive, subduing territory. Often deceitfully camouflaged as an ally, these forces are very much in opposition to any personal or spiritual progress. It's so important to make sure your attachment to any person is tested and proven (I John 4:1). These spirits, usually formed as legions, will sneak in with organized plans to dismantle God ordained unions and assignments (Matthew 8:28-34) to stop advancement!

Season after season the increased strength in opposition will make even the strongest of warriors question, "Is this even worth it?"

A Note To Every Giant Slayer:
To the Girls who won't give up, back down or step aside from the difficult assignment God assigned to you. We are those women who have been threatened and attacked by a real enemy in hopes to steal productivity from our days and sleep from our nights. Bullies who threatened our peace, who temporarily silenced our voice, and plotted against us both publicly and privately. They confused us for a minute, because they didn't show up in a red suit with horns. Instead they were dressed in business suits and ties, denim jackets and nikes, some in pearls with lace, and priestly robes. They gave no mercy! Called together in legion form, to break us, but <u>every single time the **Great I AM** showed up to our defense.</u>

You've been marked! Marked with purpose because you persevered. I know you are tired and weary, but don't you dare quit - there is an end in sight. God will cause you to rise up with supernatural strength like David, and once and for all, you will take your sword and spare not the life of your giant. And just like that, with one stone, you will go from defeat to victory, collapsed to established, from obscurity to notoriety. Every restriction to limit you, will be broken! The seeds within you will flourish, your fruit will speak and remain forever. Generations who follow you, will thank you for being brave and all the world will know your fight was never in vain!

You may feel misunderstood by those whose journey took them through grassy fields instead of violent valleys. I certainly understand, her fluffy soft slippers look nothing like your heavily worn combat boots. Well manicured hands show no resemblance to the calloused hands that have fiercely gripped your sword. If honest, you question why she got to float on a pink raft, sipping Pina Colada's poolside, while you obediently tread violent waters in areas deeper than desired. It's easy to want to give into the temptation and compare your journey to hers, especially when outsiders start judging your warlike behavior, to her refined lady like style.

Women and war? Yes, women <u>in</u> war!

Listen closely, others weren't called to walk in your war boots or hold your sword. They haven't looked into the eyes of a fierce giant that threatened your very existence and the seed you carry. Your experiences are nothing alike, so don't worry about the criticism.

You must stay focused on your assignment. There is a fierce enemy on your turf, and in this valley of decision, everything attached to you will be affected by your obedience! With this victory, you will inherit the promise and the "spoils of your enemy." Your elevation will be unstoppable as you rise to your appropriate place in His kingdom because He found you faithful. ——— Just throw the rock!

Didn't know you were a giant slayer? Me either. Didn't want to be a giant slayer? Me neither! I need to remind you, you didn't chose the battle, God chose it for you. You've been hand-picked and anointed to destroy the giant that has attempted to maim your identity, and for generations has threatened spiritual assassination.

You've been given this assignment to change generational narratives. No more excuses like, "This runs in the family" no friend, <u>this is where it stops!</u> You will be the agent of change to bring about eternal victory.

You've been assigned to fight this uncircumcised enemy, and with the promise that He will be with you. Be brave on purpose! Generations to follow are depending on you to show up and fight. With His power in you and His presence surrounding you, the giant is going down.

Pray this . . .
Lord, on my own I feel overwhelmed and afraid, but I choose to stay in this fight and embrace my assignment. I boldly take up my sword, and with courageous abandonment of my reality, I <u>move</u> forward with Your presence. I <u>will</u> annihilate every uncircumcised bully in my life. With every stone (the Words of God) released, I take down generational curses and alliances which have threatened to destroy me and my seed. No more can this enemy stand on my territory and

provoke me. Satan, the blood of Jesus Christ is against you. You are exposed and you are defeated!

I confess my sin and the sin that has gone before me. The bondage of my bloodline *(if married: and the bloodline I married in to)* shall not be my bondage. In the name of Jesus, every curse attached to my family is broken *(name those sins: pride, lack, addiction, sexual immorality, un-forgiveness, depression, sorrow, greed, anger, false humility, compromise, etc.)* This stronghold is uprooted and cancelled, forever. No longer are we a hostage to the enemy. I take back my hope, my peace, my joy, and my provision. Every area where I've experienced defeat is now reversing its order. Every blessing of the Lord He said I could have, is mine.

We are blessed My children and their children, to a thousand generations. My seed will no longer sit in cursed valleys defeated and bound, but we will stand on mountaintops blessed, anointed, favored, and restored to purpose, in the name of God Almighty! Amen.

#LetsGetReal
Sometimes you have to do it scared, until the giant falls! - Polly

#24
BEAUTY IS NOT A SIZE

"I am..." the words you decide to say after these two words can change your destiny forever. - Polly Herrin

Multi-billon dollar beauty and fashion industries both depend on the cult-like worship of what physical attributes the *"public"* deems as beautiful. Most women feel the effects of those decisions. Walk down the magazine aisle in most stores and you will find covers suggesting that beauty is found in a waist size, a designer label, a pouty lip or an eye color. These opinions are so fickle. Last season we plucked our eyebrows, wore nude lipstick, and added ombre'd highlights to our hair. This season we will fill in our eyebrows, wear muted tones of taupe on our lips, and replace highlights with extensions in deep chestnut hues. Can you even keep up with these ever changing trends? I can't.

We live in a world obsessed with physical appearance. I'm so fed up with Hollywood telling our daughters they need to be a size zero to be beautiful. *Shut up!* I'm annoyed at beauty influencers making us believe we need fake nails, fuller lips, hair extensions, spray tans, muted facial lines and bleached teeth, to qualify as attractive. Don't misquote me! There is nothing wrong with making those choices, but it is detrimental to our souls when we agree with the world that beauty is reduced to <u>only</u> the outward adornment.

Beauty is not a size! It's not a color. Beauty is not a label.

We should never let what we call beautiful be reduced to media filtered images, photoshopped body contours, or erased lines. How did we even get here? I'll tell you how: we've grown too accustomed to accepting the "likes" of others as the standard of beauty. Striving for acceptance and value from the world will send us on an unfulfilled journey. We will spend a lifetime trying to be found in the crowd, instead of being known by the Creator. This insidious cycle will break your gaze from the only eyes that will ever truly see you.

Longing to be valued and found significant, is not wrong. All of us want to be desired and loved, but we have been misguided in where to look for it! Culture keeps begging us to compare our reality with their photoshopped images, and every time we come up short. **Comparison is a hard hangover to manage.** It leaves damaging scars well after we've partaken of it. Ask the twenty-something young girl about the new set of comparisons she's wrestling with in the workplace. Instead of enjoying this exciting new season, she's overwhelmed, and feels incompetent. To escape her reality she drinks down a bottle of wine, hoping to dull the affects of comparison. Go chat with the new mother, about twelve weeks post pregnancy. She's most likely depressed and deeply agitated with her motherly figure. She deals with it by starving herself and taking diet pills. She's not concerned that her decisions affect others. Her sole desire is to be accepted. She bought into the lie too! Let's not forget to talk to the middle aged woman; she had no idea comparisons would still be a thing at her age. Her sunspots, sagging skin, and wrinkles repulse her, because most of the world wants to filter them. The natural progression of aging has become taboo and now she's hooked: hooked on fillers and facelifts to feel fancy! It doesn't stop as we mature. No, it doesn't stop unless we make it stop! Never again should we give Hollywood or beauty influencers the authority to define beauty from the other side of the screen!

The truth is, beautiful is being made in the image of God and knowing full well He created you with a purpose. It is bringing your creativity, your voice, and your gifts to the table, even if they don't look a bit like someone else's. It's time we start loving ourselves, with all our flaws and imperfections and encouraging others to do the same. A woman who knows the REAL essence of beauty accepts her voluptuous curves and belly bulge. She fulfilled her assignment to birth life through her womb. Her body is beyond amazing and she is just as beautiful after giving life as she was before. Beauty, as originally designed, is a woman who embraces her aging process. She reverently considers every stretch mark and wrinkle as a blessing from God, and the gift of another decade lived.

We need to honor God by embracing our aging bodies. Aging is not ugly! Aging is the evidence of a life beautifully lived.

Do you want to know what's ugly? I'm glad you asked. The behavior of a woman caught up in vanity, who sees herself as "better than." Her heart is tainted and her motives self seeking. You hear it in her speech. You see it in her deeds. She is self consumed and her once good intentions have been hijacked by the need to be validated. She stopped promoting others and only promotes herself, taking center stage for every event excluding the gifted women around her. Proverbs 31:30 warns us that "Charm is deceptive, and beauty is vain, but a woman who fears the Lord is to be praised."

Oh dear one, in your vain attempt to be beautiful, you have lost yourself. Sadly, you have stepped into a battle you will never win! You will forever be chasing something that will keep changing. My heart is burdened for you. I pray you run back to the Savior and find your significance in Him. His love is incomparable and His admiration gives peace and contentment this world knows nothing about.

God made you a masterpiece, unique in every way. When He designed you, every detail was considered and ultimately for His glory. He declared "You are excellent!"

He alone settled your worth, so don't go giving that authority to anyone else!

Scripture Memorization
Charm is deceptive, and beauty is fleeting; but a woman who fears the Lord is to be praised (Proverbs 31:30 NIV).

Reflection
At the end of your life, do you want those you love to remember the body you obtained, or the designer labels you wore? Will your legacy be nothing more than a physical one? Do you want your family and friends to stand by your graveside and say, "She had some amazing eyelashes and she looked incredible in a bathing suit." I doubt it!

I can promise you there are no crowns in Heaven for looking good in a swimsuit.

I realize we all have work to do to save ourselves and our culture from the consequences of its body centered, beauty driven obsession. I'm not there either, cause I'm still wearing my 3-D mascara and I love my spray tans! The truth is, it use to be so much worse. I was once obsessed with my body image, spending hours a day at the gym sacrificing time spent with my family, so I get it! Please don't think I'm suggesting we abandon healthy life styles, that is not what I am saying at all. We need balance and we can get there.

Chasing shallow validations are fleeting and unfulfilling in comparison to when I measure my worth by the scales of the Word. In Him I find unexplainable joy and validation. It is a freedom unequal to any other. It's still a process and I think it always will be. I still envy taller people and I get easily agitated when I look at my bloated belly that refuses to change. **Then I pause and force myself to remember under these Spanx, there is a body well-lived and loved! Besides, this body has done some amazing things, and so has yours!**

Now that I think of it, every inch of this body I call mine, is absolutely amazing. The achievements made with this body deserves so much more respect than the world chooses to give!

We all have work to do in valuing our bodies. We can start by laying aside the measuring sticks of comparison and instead chase after His heart, His purpose and approval. All the validation you could ever crave, is hidden in Him. By all means, take care of the temple God gave you, but don't just make the outside radiant. Let's focus our efforts just as much on keeping our souls beautiful, so the Lover of our souls will abide within us.

You and I have the power to define beauty! I say we define it by establishing the standard that beautiful lips are those which speak words that make souls stronger. Beautiful eyes see the best in others before they feel worthy. Beautiful hands carry another's burdens. Beautiful arms lift others to higher heights. Beautiful voices cheer louder for our sisters than we cheer for ourselves. You are a master piece, beautiful in every way.

Pray this . . .
Dear God, with intricate detail You created me. That overwhelms me. You certainly are all about the details! When the world tempts me to measure myself by its standards, I pray I find the strength to see this body, as Your temple, made in the image of You. Teach me to love myself. Forgive me for abusing this temple by rejecting it and speaking ill against it. I am beautiful in every way because You designed me on purpose, with purpose. I am spectacular!

On my journey to loving myself, may I be a voice of encouragement to those who also struggle in this area. Let my words bring kindness and my deeds sow generosity. I pursue to compliment first, to encourage often, and to compliment freely - Amen.

#LetsGetReal
Beauty is not a size! That is all. - Polly

#25
HUG A HATER

Go hug a hater! - Polly Herrin

Most of the male population will not relate to this devotion but I guarantee there is a "fraternity of women" who will.

Growing up I use to watch a television series, "Little House On The Prairie" that featured a snobbish, self-centered, bully named "Nelly." Nelly's father was the owner of the only successful corner store in town. Nelly was privileged and knew it. She thought highly of herself, often acting as if she were more sophisticated and educated than her peers. You would think these blessing would make Nelly kind and generous. Just the opposite. Nelly was mean on purpose and most certainly not a follower of Jesus. *She scared me - LOL!* We've all endured a "Nelly" or two. You know that spiteful woman whose mission is to keep you from entering her closed cliques and territorial spaces. With haughty eyes, an arrogant stance, and crossed arms, she lets you know real quick you're not welcome in her tribe. She's not having it!

I've personally experienced something similar. I was to attend a luncheon with others from the same organization. I made my way into the conference hall where I saw a mutual friend sitting with two of her friends. I walked over to take my seat next to her and I was completely shocked by what happened next. This so-called friend "uninvited me" by putting her purse on the chair I was about to sit in. It was noticeable. Nervously, I said hello and asked, "Are any of these seats available?" This woman wasn't about to let her friends speak for her ,and quickly she replied, "Hi Polly. No, there are no available seats here. You may want to look at the next table. It was so good to see you." Then with the fakest smile she shooed me away like she was shooing away a pestering fly. *(By the way, out of the 8 seats at her table, only 5 were occupied the entire luncheon.)*

Friends, I felt it. If she wanted me to feel it, I definitely felt it. There was no additional conversation to be had. As I rehearsed what she said and what she did, it took everything in me to fight back the tears. I couldn't wait for the program to end so I could get out of there. On the drive home, I started to consider what I could have done differently. **I should have grabbed that snotty, two-faced, fake, friend and hugged her until she couldn't breathe. But I didn't. Maybe next time.**

Sadly, many seem to think encountering "mean girls" only happens in middle school cafeterias and on college campuses where women have yet to mature. Those of us who have entered those seasons, absolutely know this is not true. *All the women over thirty said, "Amen!"* It doesn't matter your age, race, class, occupation, or personality type, you will encounter women who thrive on making you feel uninvited. A rewarding response to give would be to put your hand up in the air like you're waving, and drop all the other fingers but the middle one! Laugh if you must, but honestly I thought about giving mean girls "the middle finger" a few times. *I'm not proud of that, just being real!*

For the most part, we are good people, and the common response would be to ignore unkind words or vindictive ways. It's a worthy response, but I want to suggest a different one. What if instead you- **Hugged your hater!** I know it sounds intimidating and costly, but really what is the worst thing that could happen? Most likely your hater will be irritated that you keep pursuing her. She may resist your efforts with sinister looks and rally her "allies" near. You might try to convince yourself that it's safer to "bless" her from a distance, but if you do, the victory becomes all hers again.

Loving people involves inevitable disappointments, deep hurts, and misunderstandings. It takes great discipline to look past another's fault and still seek to give honor. And just because we are commanded to "Turn the other cheek", doesn't mean we won't feel it! Commands like "turn the other cheek" and "bless those who curse you" are far from popular and for most we assume they are impossible. But they're not impossible! In Matthew 5:44 Jesus said, "Love your enemies and bless those who curse you, do good to those who hate you, and pray for those who mistreat and persecute you." *Wow!* My goodness that's an enormous challenge. If God commands us to do it, then we must be capable to fulfill it. We can't assume it will be easy to embrace a hurting and dysfunctional world; or easy to love when it's not reciprocated, but If Jesus said we must, then He will help us.

You have the power to change the environments you occupy! Step across the lines of indifference and release love all over that woman who despises you. Pursue those who refuse you, and forgive quickly those who hurt you. Allow the power of the One that resides in you to change the one who stands against you.

Loving people is a risk, but love people anyway. You look a lot more like Jesus when you hug a hater! *Girl, we can do this.*

Scripture Memorization
...now these three remain: faith, hope and love. But the greatest of these is love (I Corinthians 13:13).

Reflection
Don't let unkind people make you unkind! Don't retaliate with the same offensive behavior. Instead, when they give you heartbreak, strife, and rejection, you can still give them Jesus.

People are often unreasonable and expect more from you than they are willing to give. Give your best to them anyway.

People may gossip about you with the intent to slander your character. Still talk good about them.

When you do good, it may be unappreciated, un-noticed or forgotten. Do good anyway.

People may be jealous of you for the public praise you receive, and the opportunities that gravitate to you. Give them praise and opportunities they have yet to find.

People may continually abuse your love and break your heart. Pray for them and do your best to love them anyway.

Pray this . . .
Lord forgive me for loving with motives! Forgive me for the seasons when I've also been mean, unkind, and judgmental. When my behavior was divisive and destructive, and I refused to see people the way You see them. I need grace for the times I disappointed You with my hardened heart and chose to live selfishly. I want to love my sisters, even when they don't love me back. I can't do this on my own, I've tried. I need Your help.

My prayer for you: Lord I pray that we become women who quickly overlook the faults of others and extend unconditional love to a world that only knows how to love with conditions! Empowered by You, we can take back hostile territories and destroy sinister missions to divide. We won't remain silent or passive any longer. We will do as You have commanded and we will expose these spirits (Ephesians 5:11). Help us to remember we do not wrestle against flesh, but we fight against spiritual things in high places. Wicked and demeaning spirits are being disrupted and all divisive plans are thwarted. With your power and authority, I break off the curse that has us fighting to compete, instead let us be women who complete one another. Build up in Your people the gift of self-control, kindness and gentleness. I pray in the days to come, we look more like You. With your help, we will - Amen.

#LetsGetReal
God still loves the one you can't stand. - Polly

#26
TURN THE PAGE

While you're still wrestling with who you are, God already knows who you can become. - Polly Herrin

The way to begin a new chapter is to end a previous chapter, and the most common way to do that is with a punctuation mark - then you turn the page! What's true in grammar is true in life, yet it seems easier said than done. It can be hard to turn the page to a new chapter when the last time you disliked the storyline and all its trouble. It wasn't romantic, prosperous or safe. Instead it was forced and fiery, and lots of broken dreams. In your disappointment, you wondered why the author would take you on such an unsettling journey. Frustrated by the plot, you lay the book out of sight. You're not having it! You resolve to never finish the story, because you cannot tolerate another chapter filled with more unknowns, heavy burdens, and sad endings. This wasn't the fairytale you signed up for.

When disappointment and unknowns surface, your life story may look nothing like what you prayed or hoped for. You question God's Sovereignty and wonder, "God, are You even writing my story, or has some other author taken over?" *I've certainly asked these same questions at times.*

Live in wastelands long enough, and the desire to escape diminishes. It's hard to still imagine that the "the best is yet to come" so you resign to a life that's less than God's best. Refusing to turn the page, you forfeit the unclaimed promises and expectant hope that lies ahead.

Isaiah 43:19 God says,"See I am doing a new thing, now it springs up; do you not perceive it? I am making a way in the wilderness and streams in the wasteland."

God is doing something new! He never intended the wasteland to be your permanent location; in fact He mandates leaving behind old mindsets, and negative attitudes, that you've adopted as normal. Discouragement keeps you believing this is how it's always going to be. Courage is willing to believe there is better coming.

Please, don't forfeit a God ordained miracle because you refuse to turn the page. You may suggest, I'm not in refusal mode but I believe God disagrees with you, because right there in the middle of His promise in Isaiah 43:19 He asks, **"Do you not perceive it?"** This question identifies unbelief. As if God knew your fragile emotions in wasteland areas would cause you to question the security of His promise.

God is so much more aware of your concerns than you are. He sees these places of unfruitfulness. . . places where you've continued to invest and have seen no real growth. Maybe in these wastelands you've even lost some things: lost a relationship, a reputation, rest or productivity. In wasteland areas your peace has been stolen, and if there remains any remnant of self-confidence, it's hanging on by a thread. The very life you once loved is now slowly on the verge of life support. Friends, that's exactly what happens when you stay in unfruitful places, where there is no one watering the soil of your soul.

God wants to move you from the wasteland to the promised land, but you have to be willing to participate. It will take extraordinary faith to release what you are trying to hold onto, and expect God can give you what you need. Like a refreshing stream that satisfies empty areas and yields new growth, God wants to restore you. He will replace chaos with order, brokenness with wholeness, and death with life; you will be rerouted from the wasteland to the promised land.

You just have to be willing to let go! Be willing to let go of this unfruitful place that isn't sufficient enough to hold the abundance of what is coming. New wine must be housed in new wineskin!

Refusing to let go of a dead thing, never brings it back to life. It only puts you at risk of becoming diseased by the deterioration. The good news is, you don't have to stay in dead places with dead words and dead dreams. Just say "yes" and allow the Author back in your story! Your next chapter holds an upgrade of living streams of water. These life giving streams will not only transform and feed *your* thirsty soul, they will flow from you, transporting eternal nourishment to others.

I promise, Jesus is worth more than anything you give up! His upgrades will far exceed your dreams, and whatever you release to Him will be counted as Holy. There's a new chapter that's better than your best dream. Go ahead, turn the page - so He can write the rest of your story.

Scripture Memorization
See, I am doing a new thing! Now it springs up; do you not perceive it? I am making a way in the wilderness and streams in the wasteland (Isaiah 43:19 NIV).

Reflection
New Year's Eve is one of the most popular holidays celebrated. I believe it's because people look forward to a fresh start. The end of a calendar year allows us to recount our accomplishments, and write out new and bigger goals. It can also be used as a time of personal reflection when we evaluate areas where we could do better. All of us have regrets which have the potential to strangle our hope to believe for better.

Every year I fall into the trap of believing that I will be able to declutter my closet. Most women reading this can relate to a full closet of duplicate items in random sizes. *Men, if you're here, I appreciate it but you can just move on to the next paragraph! LOL.* I know my female friends who've already birthed babies understand the regret of an overflowing closet holding every pair of jeans you've ever owned. The hope that your post pregnancy body will one day shrink into those jeans you wore two decades ago, is completely deflated when you recall how many years have come and gone, and your body still won't cooperate. I just counted twenty-eight pairs of jeans in my closet. I'm really bothered by this. Those twenty-eight pairs of jeans are another reminder that I have not met my goal. To some that may seem like a very shallow regret, but it's real to me. Maybe a better example would be regrets over wasted moments.

When you get to a certain age in life, wasted moments become more clear. Wasted moments spent scrolling through social media, instead of playing with the kids. Wasted moments making sure you have a cleaner house than a cleaner soul. Wasted moments sitting idle in doubt instead of embracing the challenge with faith. I've found mishandled opportunities are the regrets I rehearse most often!

I've been standing on stages since my mother took me to a "Sound Of Music" audition in 4th grade! (I was selected for the part of Marta and my love for the performing arts was ignited.) For the next eight years, until I graduated from high-school I continued developing my talents on stage with other lead roles. After graduating from college, God allowed me to further develop my public speaking skills as an employee with Microsoft. I was employed as a software trainer, and travelled the Southeast teaching top level executives. But these experiences were just the catalyst that would equip me with the confidence I would need to eventually participate in my God-given assignment: **to stand on stage and use my voice to share the message of Jesus!**

At the same time I was growing in my experience on stage, I had an equaled desire to write. I started writing decades ago. Journal entries, bible studies, prayers for my children, potential books and even long-term dreams were printed and carefully stored away in six, hot, pink, plastic containers. These brightly colored boxes housed everything I'd ever written and were once described as, **"a cocoon of hidden possibilities."** Hidden and out of sight they remained, except when these containers moved with us from state to state, home to home. Almost every time I picked one of these boxes up to move it, something inside of me would leap with excitement about the possibility these potential books could be published to encourage others. At the same time, my joy was short-lived and quickly replaced with embarrassment and shame. <u>Friends, failing tenth grade English has been one of the hardest things for me to get over.</u> The enemy continues to target my self confidence and uses this failure against me repeatedly. Fear was winning.

The fear of failing always suffocates the potential, which ultimately turns into wasted opportunities.

With every year that passed, it got easier to believe it was too late for me, and it was my own dang fault! Today, I regret letting fear sabotage my opportunities. I regret putting other people's projects before my calling. I regret not believing in myself as much as I believed in others. I regret every wasted season when I failed to seize vital opportunities and a gazillion moments to make better choices.

The enemy is good at getting us to live in the past instead of having an expectation for a better future. His streamlined effort to flood your mind with memories of failing moments and wasted moments, I can promise you, will remain on a rhythm of repeat. If he can keep you rehearsing what you lost, what you broke, what you let slip away, you won't have hope to believe what God can still do. *The devil is a liar!* **Sometimes you have to pronounce a benediction on your yesterday so you can start walking into your tomorrow. You survived it, now move on, stronger and wiser!**

The publication of this book seems late to me, and I almost talked myself out of it again. Truth is I've talked myself out of putting these words in print at leas a thousand times. Even to get it to print was not without setbacks and resistance on so many levels. Yet, finally, here it is! Today, instead of focusing on the time wasted, I choose to remember God is not limited by time, He is time. I have committed to turning my regrets into potential by partnering with Him. This "rhema" word has been released in His time, and I declare it will not return void.

If you feel regret today, I want to encourage you to let it go. Right now in this moment. None of us are perfect and we do not act perfectly, give yourself some grace. Besides, what good does it do you to hold onto regret, shame, and guilt? It never gets us to fruitful places! God can manage your regrets and even repurpose them; you just have to be willing to exit your wasteland and talk a walk in faith, towards the promise.

God plans to write the "next chapter" of your story. Oh dear child of God, "If you know how to give good gifts to your children, how much more will your Father in Heaven give good gifts to those who ask Him (Matthew 7:11)! Go ahead and turn the page - It's time for a new chapter.

Whatever is ahead will be better than anything you leave behind. Your latter shall be greater (Job 8:7).

Pray this . . .
God, I receive the promise of Your word. I release all the wasteland places of my life to You. Replace all the things that have the potential to misalign me from purpose. I want Your desires to be my desires. I give you permission to remove what has stalled my growth and hindered my ability to hear from You. Remove what is not beneficial to my future. I may bleed, and surely it will hurt, but I am willing. I give You reign over my dreams, my desires, my plans, and even my expectations! You Reign above it all. I trust in Your goodness that you are making streams in the desert. Amen.

#LetsGetReal
God never said you had to stay in the valley, He said you get to walk through it. - Polly

#27
ENDURE THE PRUNING

Don't be upset when you're rejected. Good things are rejected all the time by people who can't afford them. - Author Unknown

Through the years, God has ordered some divine connections into the lives of my family. Providentially initiated by God, these relationships have been crucial for the next step in our journey. *I appreciate them so much!* I remember a time when my husband and I sat with a couple we had only admired from a distance. Toward the end of our time together, they felt impressed to tell us, "The parts of your ministry that were bulldozed over, was the work of the enemy. God wants you to know, He allowed it, but He promises to take the rubble and rebuild it, even better. Your latter will be far greater!"

Goodness, what a word! If you will listen, God will speak to you in a season when only He could accurately pinpoint the details you needed to encourage you to stay the course, stay in the fight because He will bring good from it!

Demolition is definitely not as enjoyable as building, but it is necessary. When things are leveled to the ground it can feel frightening. These unknown seasons when you can't fix it, or restore it, requires faith to trust what God is doing is for your good. In hindsight we always see He was in control orchestrating the pruning, but it's never easy. Webster's definition of pruning is, "To cut away or remove unnecessary parts; to remove dead or living parts from a plant, so as to increase fruit or flower production or to improve its form."

When we lived in Florida we had several palm trees on our property. What Floridian doesn't? One season we noticed our Bird of Paradise palm started decaying. You may not know this, but this palm is expensive. Although I didn't want to risk loosing the investment, I figured if God said pruning was good, it had to be necessary. Grabbing the axe, I leveled that baby to the ground!

At first it looked like I made a huge mistake; but those of you who are avid gardeners know what happened next. Within a few months, new growth appeared and within a year, it stood taller and more beautiful than it did before it was pruned. Pruning the palm proved to be beneficial.

Jesus talked about pruning in John 15:1-2 saying, "I am the true vine, and my Father is the gardener. He cuts off every branch in me that bears no fruit, while every branch that does bear fruit He prunes so it will be even more fruitful."

Sometimes you won't recognize the "rotting and decay" until the damage has fiercely set in, and when decay or corruption is left unchecked it has the potential to bring destruction or even death to the living thing. It's the same with the attachments you allow in your life. God tell us to not let our heart's be deceived and protect against the things that will ruin your harvest (I Corinthians 15:33). If He warns us that our hearts will deceive us, it is utterly important that we ask Him to keep us protected, and be willing to allow Him to remove whatever needs to go. **God will always prune you, before He lets it ruin you.** His pruning may feel uncomfortable, insensitive, and costly, but whenever He removes something, it was needed. He knows exactly what to prune for the fulfillment of the promised harvest.

Character discernment is a valuable tool for avoiding toxic entanglements. We should ask God for this gift. You see, when people enter your life, they don't just bring their bodies, they bring their spirits. It's simply not enough to evaluate what we see on the outside, but we must follow Christ's command (I John 4:1) "To test the spirits to see if they are from God." Pay attention and monitor relationships that deplete your emotional energy. Be aware of those that restrict your effectiveness, and watch out for those who display jealous tendencies.

Not everybody should have access to you, and when God removes them from your life don't go chasing them down. Trying to restore what God has removed is disobedience. God only restores what He intends for you to have not what you tried to hold on to.

Scripture Memorization
I am the true grapevine, and my Father is the gardener. He cuts off every branch of mine that doesn't produce fruit, and He prunes the branches that do bear fruit so they will produce even more (John 15:1-2 NLT).

Reflection
Years ago someone publicly berated my friend *Beth* on her social media page. I assume I was the first to see it, because when I texted her to tell her that a mutual friend of ours just put insidious comments on her wall, she had no idea. She responded with a text: "Polly, I'm still at work. Would you log into my account and delete the comments, please?" That I did.

Anyone who knew *Beth* would be shocked to see such public disrespect. *Beth* was loving and overly generous. She also happened to be one of my best friends, so I was a little defensive and ready to protect her. In the days to come, the public intent to slander her character increased. Having a hard time managing the hurt, I made myself available to help her in anyway I could. One day, while our kids were swimming, she and I were cutting up watermelon. I raised the knife in the air and shouted, "*Beth*, I am willing to give up all my pastoral rights to defend and protect you, should you desire. We can hit her tires today!" I was eager to cheer her up, and it worked!

I asked *Beth* how she planned to handle this broken relationship. I was shocked when she didn't respond with, "Yeah let's go slash her tires." Instead, she shared something so profound and wise, I'll never forget it. She said, "I decided I/m not going to give it another thought." I wash shocked. I replied, "Wow, how do you do that?" Beth explained that she prayed about the entire event. She told God how shocked and hurt she was and immediately she felt God said to her, "*Beth* consider this rejection as My protection." Now I know many of us have already heard that coined phrase, but this was back in the early 90's. It was and the first time I ever heard it and obviously it hasn't been the last. It's quite the treasured quote, at one point I even thought about getting it tattooed on my arm. *LOL!* In that moment, sitting poolside eating watermelon, my friend preached one of the greatest messages I ever heard. It changed my life.

So many times I wish I had responded in the same way to people who walked away or ended the relationship without ever acknowledging me or my family. This has been one of my greatest struggles! As a Christian, I've often felt the burden to keep a friendship alive and I assumed it was my fault if the relationship failed. However, I'm learning when I invite God to monitor my relationships, He is more invested than I am. He will protect me at all costs!

Feel a loss in your life right now? A career lost? An opportunity forfeited? A relationship broken? God heard the conversations when you weren't around. He doesn't play! He provokes, protects and prunes. Rejection is just God's protection, so don't question what and who He removes.

Your good Father sees the potential fruit on your vine. His "cutting away" of some things will bring astounding growth. It may hurt. I need to rephrase that - It will hurt. Mourn and grieve the loss. Allow God to heal the torn place that happens when He prunes us, but don't stay there too long because new growth is coming. Growth beyond your expectations. Growth that will display His glory!

Pray this . . .
Lord, there are areas in my life that have the potential to cause destruction. Sometimes they are hidden and discretely camouflaged, but You see beyond the mere surface of things. You know what lies beneath. Any spirit not aligned to Your will, I give you full reign to remove. No more will I nurture disruptive behaviors that have the potential to misalign me from Your purpose. Diabolical plans sent to destroy my harvest are severed to the root. Cut it off! My family is grafted into the Vine, and every spiritual blessing is ours. We will flourish in the courts of our God and our lives will bring honor to your name.

As I am seeking Your guidance for alignments and assignments, bring to my life God ordained relationships that promote Your Kingdom purposes. Target me for Kingdom assignments, connections, talents, provision, and creativity that will assist in fulfilling Your providential will.

I don't always feel this way, but today I can praise You Lord for all the pruning You have given over the years. Now looking back, I know it was for my good. I agree with Your Word, that new growth and an abundant harvest will be the benefits of Your pruning. With expectation and praise, I will exalt you even when I see and feel the loss. You are good. You are faithful. Your ways are perfect. Amen!

#LetsGetReal
Sometimes a cut off isn't personal, it's spiritual. - Polly

#28
THIS IS NOT THE SEASON

We can't even entertain the thought that God won't be faithful. We know He will. The question to consider, "Will we be faithful to Him?"
- Polly Herrin

Our world is in a chaotic upheaval and seems to be spiraling out of control. In the last decade we have renamed marriage from its original intent between a husband and a wife. We have legalized third term abortions *(not that any abortion is justified in God's book)* and are now okay with transgender bathrooms *(we're definitely not okay, we just got duped into it.)* We honor athletes over hard working dads! We call transgenders brave for "coming out of the closet," when the brave still remain those who risk their lives to stand on foreign soil to protect our freedoms! We give honor to all the wrong things, and mostly to the wrong people. Our culture stands to salute celebrities, but stays seated when the symbol of freedom, our flag, is carried on the field. Civil unrest is on the rise and "One nation under God" is being brutally attacked and some want it removed.

As for me, my allegiance will always be to God. No mater what they threaten to remove.

What saddens me most, are self proclaimed Christians who are taking opposing sides to the biblical truths of God's Word. Folks, the Word of God isn't up for debate. We cannot decide, based upon our own desires, what is truth and what is not. That's blasphemy. Yet still today, right is called wrong and wrong is now somehow right. Do we even have to wonder why America is on a slow decline to becoming a "Godless" nation?

I remember not too long ago, when our forefathers use to take a knee in prayer closets until God answered their prayers. They knew the meaning of spiritual fasting as the way to God's response. It wasn't too long ago when we attended weekly bible studies outside of worship and sacrificed television and ball games, to prioritize family devotions.

I remember when we observed and honored Holy Communion as a sealed covenant of redemption and we did it in remembrance of Him. We embraced God's Word as "absolute truth" and forsaking our fleshly desires, we did our best to live by it.

Now the Church has digressed becoming self seeking and self absorbed. *How can you say that, Polly?* Look at our schedules. Look at what we prioritize. Are we faithful to God only when it's convenient? Do we fit Him in, only if and when we can? Answering that for myself, was and still is a humbling experience.

To keep myself accountable I often I have to return to what Jesus said in Matthew 7, "On that day many will say to me, 'Lord, Lord, did we not prophesy in your name, and cast out demons in your name, and do many mighty works in your name? And then will I declare to them, 'I never knew you; depart from me, you workers of lawlessness.'" Jesus didn't say there would be only a few, or a handful —- Jesus is saying that on judgment day many people who thought they were following Jesus, and honoring Him with their lives, will discover they really were not.

"I never knew you; depart from me," are three words I fear on judgment day. To be separated from Jesus means to be sentenced to Hell. **Please hear my heart.** This is not a dress rehearsal, this is *real* life. I feel an urgency in my spirit as I pen these words today, that America has changed, and we are no better for it. We call ourselves Christians, when in fact, to be a "Christian" is to be Christ-like. Jesus requires more than talk and good intentions, He requires obedience. We've convinced ourselves we are good, but we are not good (Romans 7:18). There is no good in us - we need a Savior!

Joshua scolded the Israelites for not obeying the Lord (Joshua 24)! He even went so far as to label them evil, for being complacent and selfish. Then Joshua stood before the assembly and commanded them to make a choice, **"Choose this day for yourselves whom you will serve"** and then with the famous words, **"But as for me and my house, we will serve the Lord"** Joshua rested his case! We see this popular saying plastered all over coffee cups and tee shirts. It's been used on wall hangings, and as hashtags. Some have even tattooed it on their arms. But I wonder do we really understand the weight of its commitment?

Are you a follower or just a fan? This is not a question to treat lightly as it has severe consequences to answering it wrong. I'm not trying to make you doubt your faith or imply you are not a Christian. I am only wanting you to reflect and answer the question for yourself - *Am I a follower of Jesus?* **Eternity is a very long time to get it wrong!**

I pray we get it right. *I pray I get it right!* We need to go back to our first love, when we prioritized our calendars with Kingdom assignments, and fought for biblical principles, regardless if we fought alone. If we would willingly go back to allowing scripture to correct us, and direct our paths how different this journey would be. Back to the days when we were less offended when the pastor preached about sin. We understood it was really God's message to us, the children He loves, and He desires that none of us perish.

This life on earth is temporary! Social media "kings and queens" will one day fall from their thrones and disappear. Politicians and lawmakers will be lifted up and then taken down. Nations will be elevated and then destroyed. Heaven and Earth will pass away, but His Word, **the only Authority**, will remain forever, and we will be judged by it (John 12:48). God I pray we get it right.

Scripture Memorization
Yet I hold this against you: You have forsaken the love you had at first. Consider how far you have fallen! Repent and do the things you did at first. If you do not repent, I will come to you and remove your lampstand from its place (Revelation 2:4-5 NIV).

Reflection
Friends, this has been an easy devotional to write. **Honestly, I have been tempted to remove this devotional three times, and replace it**

with something more appealing to my readers! But God wouldn't let me. Please know I am just the messenger, the Message is His.

I never want to sound argumentative and uncaring as I know there may be one who will read this devotional who struggles to even believe the Word of God. I understand. I promise if we were sitting across the table from one another, I would stay as long as it took to hear your heart and how you've been broken by theology and religious protocol. <u>I hear you.</u> You feel rejected instead of accepted. Please forgive us. We don't want our words to condemn you. **The gospel was meant to convict and redeem, but never condemn (Romans 8:1)! Jesus' sole purpose was to have a relationship with you.**

And so on the other side of your argument would be *me*. I believe the entire Word of God as inspired by God, and I'd hope to convince you of the same. It is the absolute truth, and I would give my life for it, but I don't hate you for believing different. I just want to share what Jesus has done for me. I would tell you how His Word has encouraged me, inspired me, strengthen me, protected me and kept me. I would do my best to explain that His Word has power but it is drenched in love. His Word is the Truth, and by it, we will be set free.

Please don't write me off. I promise I will still love you, if you disagree, We can still be friends, can't we?

<u>To the believers:</u>
To those who believe the Word of God as absolute truth, then why aren't we living like it? I pray we never live complacently as a "fan" but we make a concrete decision to **follow** Jesus for the rest of our lives.

This is not the season to become complacent or passive.
This is not the season to let media tell us what is truth and what is not.
This is not the season to go back on your word.
This is not the season to put anything above or before Jehovah God.
This is not the season to excuse ourselves from the House of God.
This is not the season for passive parenting.
This is not the season to stop saving money.

This is not the season to spend selfishly.
This is not the season to forsake His Word.
This is not the season to passively conform to cultural relativism.
This is not the season to agree that church is non-essential.
This is not the season to follow public opinion.
This is not the season to avoid the truth.
This is not the season to plead the fifth.
This is not the season to stop praying.
This is not the season to live for applause.

This is the season to pursue God with all your heart, soul, mind, and strength. To watch and pray; to be alert and ready. And to stand up for Truth, even if that means you lose the popularity vote! It's the season to re-commit to raise your children in Holy fear of God, serving Him sacrificially, and worshipping Him corporately, because there isn't allowance for another season to be wasted. This is the season to know the Word, speak the Word, defend the Word, and share the Word, with a lost and compromised world. <u>Jesus is coming soon!</u>

The world has enough women easily influenced by culture who are building earthly treasures and worn slap-out trying to do it. We need a remnant of women to rise up and do hard, unpopular, Holy things! We need the remnant to come out of hiding, join together in unity, and live our lives to build eternal treasure, bringing back honor to our King!

Pray this . . .
Oh God, we need you in America! Have mercy on us. Forgive us Lord, we have disrespected Your Word, and disregarded Your truth. We've put other things before You. We've made excuses for ourselves, and justified our actions. I am sorry Lord, I repent. Cleanse this earthly temple. Make it a reverent place again, where You show up to meet me, fill me, and teach me. If my heart or motives are unpleasing to you, show me the error of my ways. Give me a heart to do Your will, despite my desires. In hard times and with hard people, I pray I have the confidence and courage to speak the truth in love. I will teach Your commandments to my children and their children! It will be a priority in

our home. Worship will be reinstated and I will honor the Sabbath and keep it Holy. Your Word will be loved and reverenced by me and as I seek You, revelation will fill me.

As for me and my house we will serve the Lord. All of our days we will dwell in Your House forever. We will follow wherever You go - Amen!

#LetsGetReal
Discernment will be premium in this season. You've got to have wisdom to know which are constants and which are variables. - Polly

#29
DELAYS & DETOURS

There is nothing that can stop what God has guaranteed!
- Polly Herrin

For more than four-hundred years, God's people were bound in slavery by Pharaoh. God sent ten plagues to punish the Egyptians for holding God's people hostage. It was a long time of bondage! When Pharaoh finally let them free, they celebrated, but it didn't last long. Pharaoh changed his mind and sent chariots to chase down the Israelites. Their leader Moses knew their enemies were quickly approaching, so he sought God for direction. Leading a caravan of about six-hundred thousand people to freedom is no easy task. With so much at stake, you would presume Moses would take them on the shortest route, and down a familiar road, but the Bible says Moses followed God's directions and rerouted them through the desert (Exodus 13). It was definitely the hardest route and to any one it would seem foolish. To make matters worse, their obedience landed them at the Red Sea, a blockade, a dead end! The Israelites didn't keep quiet about it. They blamed Moses and declared this route would be the death of them.

Let's pause and really imagine the enormity of this moment. A caravan of desperate people finally escaped centuries of slavery only to find themselves standing at a dead end, with an army of enemies behind them. A Red Sea - The End! No doubt they were afraid and felt hopeless, and without a way of escape, mothers, fathers, and children would perish to their deaths. How could this be? How could God allow such a moment of complete turmoil and chaos?

We have to empathize with Moses. Really can we fault him like his followers, for ending up in front of the Red Sea?

I love the bravery Moses displayed. Despite what he thought, what he saw, or what he heard Moses continued to obey God! When he is told to stretch out his staff over the water, I'm sure Moses thought, really God, is that all you got? *LOL*.

As we read the order of these events, we have an advantage to this story, because we get to read the end. We can cheer Moses on, and bet the "staff move" will have its benefits, but Moses had no idea what would happen next. He just decided to believe God, regardless. He had seen His faithfulness before and he trusted that whatever came next, God was still in control.

God is the God of grand reversals. You know what happened - a took place! **God turned the Red Sea into a red carpet making a way for the Israelites to walk across dry ground safely to the other side.** God doesn't make mistakes. It was always God's plan that Moses and his followers would go <u>through</u> the Red Sea. The limitations they saw God never acknowledged! He intended to use that water to drown every single one of their enemies.

Sometimes God's ways feel like the longer way, and the harder way. He may direct your steps into a lion's den, a prison, a pit, or some other avenue that feels like a wrong turn, but there are no wrong turns when God is leading.

The hopeless situation you find yourself in today may cause you to question, "Did God really allow this?" The answer is a resounding *YES*! He may not have caused it, but He definitely allowed it. God isn't limited to your finite plans nor is He confined to the laws of the land. He operates on another level. He doesn't need your permission to do the impossible, He just needs your obedience and your faith!

Every impossible situation is still controlled by His governing, so hang on friend, 'cause He's about to pull out the miracle that overrides the impossible. Watch and see!

Scripture Memorization

Trust in the Lord with all your heart and lean not on your own understanding; in all your ways acknowledge Him, and He will make your paths straight (Proverbs 3:5-6 NIV).

Reflection

There have been seasons when I dreamed big and acted in big faith, and in other seasons, I barely had enough faith to pray. When things don't go as planned we can easily "lean into our own understanding" and try to make sense of the process. Faith requires us to trust in the Lord and resist the temptation to have to understand.

I love those times when right in the middle of a confusing season, God speaks clearly. That happened for me, like this.

My friend Lori called a few days before my birthday to let me know, my gift was in the mail and it was to arrive on Thursday. Thursday came and went, with no sign of the package. Honestly, I forgot about it, and she did too. Fast forward almost five months later, Lori came to visit. We greeted one another in the driveway, and before she even took her luggage from the car, she grabbed something from the front seat. With the silliest, amusing, smile, she handed a package to me and said, "Here's your birthday gift! You didn't think it would ever get here, did you?" The package was dirty, damaged, and completely covered up with written dates and states denoting where it had travelled. Looking closer, we observed it went to four different locations before the package made its way back to Florida where the last written note said, "Return To Sender." Lori said, "I couldn't risk putting it back in the mail, I just assumed it would be better to hand deliver it to you. Happy Birthday, Friend!"

My birthday gift may have gone through a course of unplanned stops to get to me, but it got to me! It may have detoured, and transferred hands a couple of times even landing in the wrong place, but my name was on the package. It was on it's way to me because <u>it was always mine!</u>

The Bible says in Galatians 6:9, "Let us not grow weary in doing well, for in due season you will reap if you do not lose heart." That word "due" in Webster's dictionary is defined as "an obligatory payment." It doesn't imply it *may* happen, or it *could* happen, rather it is a confirmation that it <u>will</u> happen! God has a due moment for every promise He made. The enemy may have tried to convince you it's never going to arrive, don't you believe him. **There is nothing that can stop what God has guaranteed!** It may not arrive on the day you expected, but the promise He gave is in formation, and it won't miss you!

Pray this . . .
God, You said You have good plans for me. Even plans to prosper me. Today those don't feel very prosperous or even good. Honestly, this detour and delay has me confused. I'm not sure what to do or which way to go. I'm afraid and anxious. Please settle my heart and let my soul be at rest in Your Sovereign ways. Grow my faith to declare You will turn this mess into a miracle, regardless how I feel, or what I see. Give me determination to endure every detour, knowing it could be positioning me for the miracle that's on the way. You are the God of miracles. You are a Way-Maker! Nothing is impossible for you. You will come through again. Regardless of what it looks like in the natural, I will lift my hands to Heaven and praise Your name. I am confident in who You are, and my hope is secured in Your faithfulness - Amen.

#LetsGetReal
Don't confuse losing confidence in your ability and losing confidence in God's. They are definitely not the same. - Polly Herrin

#30
SOCIAL MEDIA LIES

I hope you find a <u>love so loud</u> that it silences all your insecurities. - Polly Herrin

In a world where followers and likes can seem like rock-solid proof of a person's worth, you don't have to take the bait.

I believe, social media has become one of the enemy's greatest weapons, to provoke unhealthy comparisons. Statistics show that social media obsession can lead to low self-esteem, insignificance, depression, and isolation. *Why is this?* I believe it's because as we are constantly scrolling we are continually comparing, and what we tend to compare is unequal. All of us have been guilty of comparing our unfiltered life to another's "hight-light reel," which can leave us feeling less than.

We've all heard the term "selective posting." It's the process we use to determine what photos make the feed and which ones don't. Most of us have all participated in some level of this behavior, because I don't see many friends posting photos and videos of sibling rivalry, or broken hearts. Rarely will you find images of dirty cars, unmade beds, burnt dinners, or clogged toilets - *gross*! But folks, every once in a while you have to unclog the toilet! *Come on friends, don't get all self-righteous on me now, you have toilets that need unclogged too! #LetsGetReal*

All of us have a few unglamorous moments in our past which, if given the chance, we'd like to undo. Yet somehow we conclude the girl we compare ourselves with, doesn't have any moments she'd like to redo. *She's perfect.* Truth is, *Her* social media feed may not reflect it but she's been filtering too. <u>We all filter</u>. In reality she's extremely anxious, broken, fearful, and intimidated despite the confidence she displays on her feed. She cried herself to sleep last night because she feels insignificant and excluded. Her perfectly contoured body has been a result of diet pills she's been popping for decades. Starving herself has become her normal. She's convinced her body is the only thing that makes her husband stay... *I'm grieving for Her. Are you?* You'd never know it, but she's flat out broke flying coast to coast paying top dollar to the best surgeons in the beauty industry. **She's been nipped and tucked more times than a Kardashian!** And here we are comparing our bodies to an upgraded version that's been paid for. Friends, there is nothing wrong with nipping and tucking, especially if you have the money to pay cash for those procedures! I'm just trying to unveil the ridiculous lies we tend to believe as we sit on the other side of the screen. More times than we are willing to admit the filtered images we view make us despise the bodies God intricately designed to house our beautiful souls. If we are not cautiously careful, we will become obsessed with a perfected image that somebody paid for!

We can become so envious of everything about *Her*, that isn't even *real*. She didn't lie, Social Media did!

Someone once said, "Comparison is the thief of joy." Absolutely it is. Comparison will make you see differently, think differently and react irrationally. **Comparison is a trick of the enemy to get us to be attentive in areas that sometimes aren't even authentic and it's working! Maybe if we recognized this insidious obsession as an unfulfilling lie, we would stop chasing after "fake fairytales" that have us resenting our real lives.** Every infatuation with *Her* can skew our perception of life, and cause us to miss out on the beautiful unfiltered moments that make this journey amazing.

My friend, you are made in the image of an awestruck God. You don't have to try to be something you're not. God sees the unfiltered you and He doesn't love you any less. You may be "messy" to the world, but He sees your potential and promises to use it.

I know it's frightening to expose and unveil yourself before Him. *You're afraid, I hear you.* But *this* love looks nothing like the love from those who may have mishandled your heart in the past. He won't shame you. He won't isolate you. He won't love you with conditions, and I promise,

He will never walk away. No, He rushes toward you, leans in to embrace you, and just as He did for the Samaritan woman, He will go out of His way to find you.

He sat on a well and waited for her. He could have been anywhere, out to lunch with the disciples, in the synagogue, on the hillside preaching to the masses, but <u>she was His priority</u>! A discarded woman, not valued by many. **She was un-named, but she was never unnoticed. Her life was filled with broken and filthy moments that made her believe beauty and restoration were impossible, until she saw Him and He saw her! She felt it.** Like no other feeling she'd ever experienced, Heaven came down and met her. She was never the same. Meeting this man named Jesus, *a Living Well* who became an overflow of love and grace, changed her life. This meeting quenched every dry place in her soul, and gave her unexplainable hope that would never expire. On this day she encountered *"The Well"* that never runs dry. Full of Jesus, she became a "living testimony" restored, healed and whole. You can too!

I pray you see Him. He sits today waiting for you. Not at a well, but in the sunrise of a new morning. He promises new mercies are available today, and the depths of His grace are as deep as an ocean. Stop scrolling, and start seeking Him. In His presence, the cravings of your inner soul will be more than satisfied. He will pour Himself out like a drink, to fill you to overflowing (2 Timothy 4:6). You can absolutely live unfiltered and still be loved by God!

There is a world that needs to know God doesn't look for perfect people to share His message. God uses imperfect people who know all too well the extravagance of His grace and through their imperfections have testified that His love, radically and eternally, changed their lives.

We need you to be you. Not the filtered you, but the filled you!

Scripture Memorization
I will lift up mine eyes unto the hills, from whence cometh my help. My help comes from the Lord (Psalm 121:1-2 NIV).

Reflection

When we willingly hit the "follow" button on social media, we are telling someone, "I want a glimpse into your life." We know that what we see is often curated with intentionality to lure you in for the *likes* and *loves*. But social media can cancel you just as quickly as it promoted you.

Unapologetically we've embraced this filtered way of life: we endorse the elevation of perfection because the world rarely gives sympathy to anything less. As a result, we've reduced "love" to transactional likes, shares and follows. If we allow it, social media can become a cycle of constant defeat that begs for our attention and easily detours us. Some glances can amplify your insecurities and others will expose jealousy. When we don't set realistic boundaries, we will end up searching for healing and peace in a place that was never made to provide it.

Social media lies! We are all undone and un-glamours, *as filthy rags,* without the grace and mercy of Jesus Christ (Isaiah 64:6)! The only perfect One went to the cross to pay for the sins of the imperfect, and His name is Jesus. If you find yourself weary of criticism and judgment, speculation, or rejection of any kind, remember God is not made of harsh words and broken promises. He is abundant in Presence, Purpose and Love. He never asks for perfection, He asks for relationship! Isn't that what we all are searching for? To be known, to be loved, and to be embraced.

You are more than the descriptions in your profile. And your value is not determined by the number of followers by your name, it's determined by THE ONE YOU FOLLOW.

King Solomon said it best, "God has set eternity in the human heart" (Ecclesiastes 3:11)! No matter how much your influence increases on your social media platforms, your soul will never be fully satisfied until it finds its eternal home in God.

Real love is found when we abandon all to follow Jesus - He alone is The Way, The Truth and The Life.

Pray this . . .

Lord, help me. I am sometimes obsessed with the "likes" of many. Most often I feel hurt when I am rejected by others. Social media has distracted from the overflow of Your love. Comparison has crippled me. Yet again, You remind me I don't have to do anything to earn Your love and I am so thankful I can never lose it. Bind this truth to my heart.

Give me the boldness to continue to live authentically. I want the world to see Your love is always abounding; on good days and bad days. I rebuke the mindset I have adopted that tells me I must be approved by the world, in order to gain greatness. I rebuke the lies that have me believing that influence, power and wealth are only for those sold out to themselves. Your Word promises that You give the power to gain wealth, You bring kings to positions of elevation, and You make men seen and known! As I live my life to reflect Your glory, I can be confident that You will make my ways succeed, and everything I do will prosper. It's my desire that others will find Your extravagant love, that allows imperfections. May they see that LOVE in me - Amen.

#LetsGetReal
God uses imperfect people who know all too well the extravagance of His grace. - Polly

EXTRA: THIS ONE'S FOR THE GIRLS

Dedicated to my daughter Karson, my Daughter-in-love Maddy, and also to those I have adopted as daughters.

Don't call me bossy. If I were a boy, you'd call me a leader. - Unknown

When my daughter Karson was a toddler, her father and I noticed she could be very strong willed at times, one might have called her "bossy!" She was never shy about giving her opinion. One time I had to correct Karson for throwing a stick at her brother. On her way to her bedroom, she yelled back to us, "I'm gonna own the world one day, and you and Noah can live in it." *I believed her.*

Today as I write this, she's a senior in college. Her confident ability to lead is astounding. To watch her network people together for a common cause is admirable, and her love for people is highly contagious. We were not surprised when she earned a complete four-year scholarship for her leadership skills. *You heard it right. Praise God!*

This girl is brave, confident, bold and taking territory for God.! It's always been this way: Karson lacks no faith regarding things she's convinced God told her to do.

I remember once when Karson was young she didn't want to leave church, she had a breakdown in the lobby. (Now, before I continue the story, I just want to point out that wanting to be in God's house is always good thing. Remember in the scriptures when Jesus got lost? His parents scolded Him for leaving their side but Jesus said, "I had to be about My Father's business (Luke 2:49)." I rehearsed that scripture often as a parent, because Karson always wanted to be at the Church. Still to this day she loves the House of God. Parenting can sometimes cause conflicting emotions and on this day, I didn't know whether to discipline Karson for her back-talking, or ignore it and be thankful she wanted to be in God's house. It was a typical response from Karson to try to convince me to let her stay longer, this day was no different.

Karson begged, "Momma, just leave me here!" Before I could respond, she interrupted, "Momma, *I need to stay here!* This is Jesus' house and I gotta stay here. If not, He is not going to be happy with you."

This was Karson! I can still see it vividly in my memories . . . those big brown eyes, naturally curly hair, dark Florida sun kissed skin, her tiny painted pink toes peering out of sparkling white flip flops, and swaying her hips from one side to the other! (Those who knew Karson then know exactly what I'm talking about! LOL!)

I didn't know whether to laugh, cry, spank her, or applaud her. Her entire thought process for an almost five year old was totally right, yet at the same time, all wrong. Mrs. Janie, my husband's secretary, busted out hysterically in laughter. Karson didn't like it. She really was serious and wanted me so badly to understand. She put her arm straight out, palm facing Mrs. Janie, like a crossing guard does to stop traffic, and with a stern slow voice she said, "Mrs. Janie please stop laughing." Others were now watching - isn't that what happens when you have a five-year-old acting out and you're the pastor's wife? Noah, my oldest about ten at the time, warned his little sister, "Oh my gosh Karson, you are in serious trouble!"

We have so many stories like this tucked away in our memories! We joke often with Karson to remind her how strong-willed and determined she was from the start. I've always had a sweet spot for strong-willed girls. Sometimes they've been strong to survive, other times they were strong because God knew they would need to survive later in life, and sometimes it's been for both.

A new observer made their way into the lobby. Before the crowd had a chance to swell larger, I grabbed Karson's back-pack and her little outstretched arm at the same time. Quickly gathering things and escorting my kids to the door, I was honestly trying to rescue them from the criticism I knew would be coming. But before I could get away this new observer blurted out, "Well we all know Karson gets that strong, not gonna back down attitude (BIG PAUSE) from her mother!" ***Hmmmm - no comment!***

I knew the slanted criticism was coming, but I had no idea it was coming for me this time. This person wanted me to *feel* it! Have you ever had someone want you to feel it? You know that casual criticism they slid in there at just the right time, yet always defended as an innocent joke. It was not only intended for me to hear, but it was intended to attack my worth as a parent, and that's exactly what it did. I felt it, and it lingered for months. Truth be told, my son felt it too. I believe Karson was too young to understand this negative intent, but with one look into my son's eyes, I could see his emotional concern for me.

An awkward silence filled the lobby. Mrs. Janie immediately came to the rescue, "Yes she is just like her momma, and one day Karson is going to move mountains in the spiritual realm, because she's not a quitter!" Another friend standing close by quickly agreed and spoke up, "Yes Karson will never be easily persuaded. She's going to follow Jesus boldly! She's a leader." I love my friends for rallying around us as accusations came to inflict harm to my soul, but it didn't stop the tears from rushing down my cheeks. I reached for my sunglasses to hide the tears. I was heart-broken again as well as infuriated, but I still managed to practice what I'd preached to so many other moms. My last words echoed the halls of that building when I shouted back, "Karson's name means, 'Follower of Christ!' She will absolutely follow Jesus and live for Him in bold confidence! I expect her to be a leader. She is a leader in the making."

Regardless of what the enemy intended to flow in the airways that day, God was reversing the curse with some friendly bystanders who agreed with me that Karson would use that brave personality, to one day live by faith and move mountains!

Me, well I acted real "grown up" in that moment, but I felt assaulted. When I got home, I grabbed my babies like a mother hen huddles her chicks. I reminded them, "Noah and Karson, I love you both. I love that you love Jesus. Never, ever apologize for loving Him loud and never stop believing He loves you back! You are leaders and not followers. Great and might things you will do for Him. Don't apologize for it."

To all the parents out there trying to parent a strong willed children or strong-willed teenagers, the best advice is to give them boundaries, but don't crush their spirits. **I can promise God has a reason for the inner strength these children carry! They are spiritual leaders in the making whom God WILL use to walk into dark arenas, carrying the light of Jesus!**

Fast forward, now at age twenty-one, this beautiful, brassy, strong willed, sold out leader and follower of Jesus Christ we named Karson, has turned into the most confident faith walking, talking woman of God I know! <u>Her faith is contagious!</u> <u>Her prayers touch Heaven.</u> <u>Her leadership skills are off the chart.</u> <u>She isn't afraid to speak and declare the goodness of God. She believes God for the impossible and lives expectantly that He will come through</u>. That's exactly how she landed that educational scholarship, I mentioned above. Four years of paid tuition doesn't just happen - God had a plan.

In full disclosure, my husband and I tried to convince Karson to apply to other colleges because the scholarship she was applying for was a long shot. There was only one scholarship available. Karson's response still held so much faith, "All my life you have taught me the word of God and asked me to trust Him. The very first scripture verse you made me and Noah memorize was **Proverbs 6:2 - I am snared by the words of my mouth!** Mom, Dad, this is all I have to say about it. You can snare me, or you can help declare out-loud that God is going to make a way for this to happen! I know He is going to do this and neither of you will convince me otherwise."

Fast forward . . . A few weeks later Karson's faith was put to the test when she found out the scholarship was given to someone else. The enemy never backs down or intends to let us walk into territory, and possess it without resistance.

Karson raced up to her bedroom, crying. I was in the kitchen finishing the dishes. I leaned over the sink, feeling spiritually depleted! One by one, tears rolled down my face and splashed into the sink water as I tried to understand my baby girl's faith and confidence was being shattered. I begged God to help me know the words to say to console Karson. As I was interceding for her, I could hear Karson's footsteps pacing on the ceiling above my head. And then I heard the most beautiful melody escape from her lips, "Way maker, miracle worker, promise keeper, light in the darkness, My God, that is who You are." She began to sing the lyrics to Waymaker! A few minutes in, I was down stairs on my knees joining her.

Even when this looked impossible and hopeless, Karson's faith was still strong! My little faith, mixed and blended with her extravagant faith, began to be a symphony of allegiance to a God who <u>DOES NOT FAIL!</u>

Can I tell you, the atmosphere changed in our home that day because Karson wouldn't allow her circumstances to dictate her emotions! She believed God would keep His promise, and He absolutely did! Forty-eight hours later, Karson received a phone call from the Dean of Students awarding Karson the scholarship. You see behind the scenes, a well deserved student named Karis received the leadership scholarship. Usually this scholarship is only given to one incoming freshmen, but as it turned out, the Dean and those on the scholarship board, felt so strongly that Karson also deserved the scholarship. <u>They made an exception and did what had never been done before in the history of Emmanuel College, awarding *two* freshmen the scholarship!</u>

(Praise Break!) Come on somebody - if that doesn't get your attention, I don't know what will.

You see, Karson was never giving up easily, because had seen the faithfulness of God many times and in many areas of her life. She wasn't about to back down. **Her faith exploded in the face of hopelessness.** She was more than confident God would make a way and nobody could tell her differently.

Now decades later, I wish I could go back in time to our church lobby in Florida and hear that critical spirit come at us again with, "Well we all know where Karson gets that strong, not gonna back down attitude . . .

from her mother!" The critical comment intended to hurt me, now could not be more honoring to me.

Why is it that society deems outspoken boys as leaders, but labels outspoken girls as bossy?! Why is it that middle school girls are "emotional" for voicing their objective opinions but middle school boys, arguing the same facts, are "finding their voice"! Okay and let's go there while I'm addressing the inconsistencies. A female who openly takes a stand on public stages giving her opinion when you didn't ask for it, is labeled the "B-word!" That same aged human, but opposite in gender, could say the same thing and he is considered a male hero, an independent thinker, and a positive contributor to society.

Please, why can't *SHE* be that too?

Who are we to judge which gender we should applaud that exhibits a strong voice, strong opinions or strong leadership skills? God is the creator of all human beings and some personality traits we learned, but some were written into our DNA!

Ladies, how many times have you been criticized because you stated your opinion, found your voice, or stood up for yourself or someone you loved? If God is Sovereign, then why should you try to change how He made you and how can you not embrace the life experiences He allowed you to walk through?

I know there are many women who will read this who weren't born confident, but through tragic life experiences have gained heroic strength. Their hearts have endured so much heartache because they were forced to survive situations they can't even talk about. Women who have walked through things that should have made them crazy, or worse, put them six feet under - but they survived long enough for God to step in and rescue them. Not without, of course, the scars to prove it!

GOD MADE HER! Strong, confident, brave, faith-walking, faith talking, fearless leader that you would like to so easily discredit, because she's a little brassy, sassy, and talks like a survivor. Thank God for women who stand their ground in the face of severe attacks to overcome! We should applaud women just as loudly as we applaud men, who fight the urge to sit silently on the sidelines of life, accepting anything that's handed them.

WOMAN OF GOD! You were made to win! God specifically chose the woman to give life. Nobody would be on this earth without a women. (Applaud yourself.) Every woman has purpose, but you won't fulfill it passively. So, whatever critical spirit has followed you around for the majority of your life, tell it to sit down and shut up! We will no longer be intimidated by chauvinistic spirits that want to keep us confined. God paid a high price for us and no opinion can devalue our worth. We will take the risk to save our people, despite what you call us, and what labels you assign to us. We will be about our Father's business, sacrificing our costly oil, which to you may seem wasteful. Criticize us if you feel the need, but your words will never stop our relentless praise to our King. Pouring it on His feet, we rejoice in knowing He will cherish us, forever.

There were many times I judged myself by the way others in the room valued me, but those days are completely over and they should be for you, too. I am confident in who God made me! I will walk into rooms knowing God sent me there. I will raise children and grandchildren who are confident in who God made them, and I have made it my life's mission to teach Karson and Noah to never limit their abilities, based upon man's disapproval.

It is my greatest joy to watch them soar in their callings. To see them stand with God, even if it means they may have to stand alone. I have no doubt they will do all God intended and nothing will stop them.

Scripture Memorization
God is within her, she will not fail (Psalm 46:5)!

Reflection

Karson, don't you dare change yourself for the world! Don't dim your beauty or talent because others are threatened by it. Don't disown the anointing on your life to make others feel more valuable. Don't diminish your calling so others can find theirs. Bring them with you if you have to, but don't you reduce yourself in order to belong! Keep making waves, my girl. Jump in deep, and don't worry about the splash that may get others wet. They will awaken to see God is in you. He created your voice to speak to dark places to bring hope and light. He created you to be a leader, not a follower, to make a lasting impact in this world for His glory. I have no doubt you will do exactly that.

I love your sassy, bossy, confident unwavering, faith walking, talking self! When people say, "She's so much like her mom" - I SMILE - knowing you were made for what is ahead! Go get everything God promised you, my Girl. I'll be cheering you on every step of the way.

I love you, a million times circled to the heavens and back...(and so does your Father).
XO, Mom

Pray this . . .
God, if I have judged others wrongly, forgive me. I can't see the entire picture of what You have allowed in their lives that will ultimately shape them for the way You intend to use them in the future. Help me always, to encourage the gifts within others.

Lord, I choose to forget those things behind me (words, deeds, and wrong intentions) that have tried to devalue my worth and threaten my success. I am made in Your image, by You, with a purpose You created me to fulfill (Psalm 138:8). My experiences, good and bad, have all influenced who I would become. I will not deny them, but I will allow them to be used by You, to develop me for the next step in this journey.

I will take the stones others have thrown at me and build a step, to the next level. I will take the hard experiences that left me broken, and allow that experience to increase within me kindness and understanding for other broken people! I will look back and remember the ways in which You remained faithful, even when I was faithless. I love you, Lord!

I will live to be all You have created me to be! In every future season of my life I will see the goddess of the Lord in the land of the living. Every seed by faith I plant, will produce an undeniable harvest that will not only bless me, but a generation who will follow. As I remain faithful under trial, You promise to take me through. I will walk victoriously and I shall overcome.

I will forever live to glorify Your name in everything that I do. Use me Lord, however and whenever You desire - Amen.

#LestGetReal
Don't diminish your beauty, talent or calling because others can't see their own. - Polly

SPECIAL THANKS

<u>MY FAMILY</u>: Torrey, Karson, Noah and Maddy, thank you for believing in me, and pushing me forward to finish this assignment. I am extremely grateful for your personal input throughout the process of publishing this book; including the layout, title and design on both the front and back covers. Your opinions matter the most to me! You are my greatest gifts and my favorite people to be with - I love you with my whole being!

* Thank you Maddy for designing both the front and back covers. Thank you Noah for leading me through the entire process of publication. I could not have done this without your help.
* Thank you Torrey and Karson for your continued encouragement. When it got tough and stressful, <u>you ate the cookies for me.</u> Ha! Seriously, your daily encouragement pushed me to finish.
* Thank you Mom (and Dad who now has his eternal reward) for giving me opportunities as a child to know Jesus. I am eternally grateful.

Note: towards the end of this project, my grandson Lion was born. I am now a *KiKi*. He is my favorite and I make no apologies about it.

<u>MY SOUL SISTERS/BOOK EDITORS</u>: Jessica & Tina, you helped me find misspelled words, missing commas, and corrected all my crazy sentences. Thank you! For decades our friendship has been solid. You've been my sounding board, always there with a word of wisdom, a solution, or a prayer. You've been the strong sister(s) I needed, who would correct me when I got off course, but you were also willing to run with me when the terrain was unknown. Thank you. I love you both. I am thankful God gave me you to travel with on this journey. I pray every hour of investment you've made in this project, God returns back to you one-hundred times on this side of Heaven.

<u>MY TRIBE</u>: (*You know who you are!*) For years you have protected me, encouraged me, and motivated me through every season. The prayers, the impartation of biblical wisdom, and the deeds of kindness you have sown into my life means so much. I would be empty without you. When

I thought my words and my voice didn't matter, you said, "Yes they do!" When I wanted to quit, you talked me out of it. You've always believed in me and cheered me on. Everyone needs family and friends like you.

<u>MY FRIENDS</u>: To every friend near and far, who encouraged me to publish my first book, you will never know the motivation your words gave me to finish this assignment (and the next one, Lord willing)! <u>This book was written with you in mind.</u> As I journeyed through the process to completion, it was not without resistance, and I would frequently rehearse your kind words of encouragement. Those words kept me motivated! Thank you for taking the time to be my friend. You add beauty to my life.

AND to the ladies I currently get to lead. Words could never accurately articulate how grateful I am for the monetary contributions you have given to assist in the publication of this devotional (happy tears). I am so honored you believed in me that much - I hope I make you proud.

<u>MY GOD:</u> Most importantly, I thank You! You are faithful. You never gave up on me, even when I gave up on myself. In difficult seasons when I lost the strength to carry on, You picked me up and carried me through. Your Word has embraced me to wholeness. You gave me the confidence I needed to believe I am worthy. Your love is incomparable like nothing I've ever experienced. The broken places of my soul that I tried so hard to keep locked away, and out of reach, You tenderly pursued and restored. **I don't deserve You God, but I'm so glad You're mine.** Wherever and whenever You allow me the opportunity, I will tell of Your extravagant love and audacious grace that completely transformed my life.

As long as I have breath . . .

Made in the USA
Columbia, SC
23 November 2021